PEOPLES
of
AFRICA

Morocco

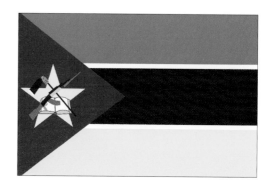

Mozambique

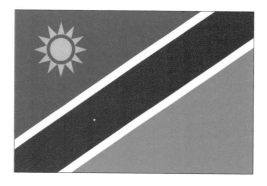

Namibia

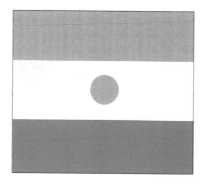

Niger

Nigeria

PEOPLES
of
AFRICA

Volume 7
Morocco–Nigeria

MARSHALL CAVENDISH
NEW YORK • LONDON • TORONTO • SYDNEY

Marshall Cavendish Corporation
99 White Plains Road
Tarrytown, New York 10591-9001

Reference Edition 2003

Consultants:
Bryan Callahan, Department of History, Johns Hopkins University
Kevin Shillington

Pronunciation Consultant: Nancy Gratton

Contributing authors:
  Fiona Macdonald
  Elizabeth Paren
  Kevin Shillington
  Gillian Stacey
  Philip Steele

Discovery Books
  Managing Editor: Paul Humphrey
  Project Editor: Helen Dwyer
  Text Editor: Valerie J. Weber
  Design Concept: Ian Winton
  Designer: Barry Dwyer
  Cartographer: Stefan Chabluk

Marshall Cavendish
  Editorial Director: Paul Bernabeo
  Editor: Marian Armstrong

The publishers would like to thank the following for their permission to reproduce photographs:
  Robert Estall Photo Library (Carol Beckwith: 376; Carol Beckwith/Angela Fisher: cover, 378, 381, 403; Angela Fisher: 356, 370); Werner Forman Archive (352; British Museum, London, UK: 388; Entwistle Gallery, London, UK: 383; Museum für Völkerkunde, Berlin, Germany: 386); gettyone Stone (Gerard Del Vecchio: 357 top; Nicholas DeVore: 357 bottom); Hutchison Library (384, 390, 391, 398 top; Sarah Errington: 392 bottom, 400; John Hatt: 374; Jeremy Horner: 354, 361 bottom; Mary Jelliffe: 355); ICCE Photolibrary (Joe Blossom: 395); Panos Pictures (Trygve Bølstad: 366 bottom; Jean-Léo Dugast: 359 top, 359 bottom, 361 top; James Morris: 393, 399; Bruce Paton: 397; Giacomo Pirozzi: 368 bottom, 372, 380, 394; Marcus Rose: 402; Chris Sattlberger: 364, 368 top; Marc Schlossmann: 362; Sean Sprague: 350, 358); Still Pictures (Adrian Arbib: 373; Mark Edwards: 392 top, 398 bottom; Carlos Guarita: 366 top, 396; Paul Harrison: 401; Gerard and Margi Moss: 369; Jorgen Schytte: 379; Hjalte Tin: 375)

(cover) A Hausa man dressed as a warrior decorates his horse for a Sallah celebration in Katsina, northern Nigeria.

Editor's note: Many systems of dating have been used by different cultures throughout history. *Peoples of Africa* uses B.C.E. (Before Common Era) and C.E. (Common Era) instead of B.C. (Before Christ) and A.D. (Anno Domini, "In the Year of the Lord") out of respect for the diversity of the world's peoples.

Library of Congress Cataloging-in-Publication Data

Peoples of Africa.
      p. cm.
    Includes bibliographical references and index.
    Contents: v. 1. Algeria–Botswana — v. 2. Burkina–Faso-Comoros — v. 3. Congo, Democratic Republic of–Eritrea — v. 4. Ethiopia–Guinea — v. 5. Guinea-Bissau–Libya — v. 6. Madagascar–Mayotte — v. 7. Morocco–Nigeria — v. 8. Réunion–Somalia — v. 9. South Africa–Tanzania — v. 10. Togo–Zimbabwe — v. 11. Index.
    ISBN 0-7614-7158-8 (set)
      1. Ethnology—Africa—Juvenile literature. 2. Africa—History—Juvenile literature. 3. Africa—Social life and customs—Juvenile literature. I. Marshall Cavendish Corporation.

GN645 .P33 2000
305.8'0096—dc21

                                                99-088550

      ISBN 0-7614-7158-8 (set)
      ISBN 0-7614-7165-0 (vol. 7)

Printed in Hong Kong

06   05   04   03   6   5   4   3   2

Contents

MOROCCO

MOROCCO IS A COUNTRY IN NORTHWESTERN AFRICA, bounded in the north by both the Atlantic Ocean and the Mediterranean Sea.

Narrow, fertile plains lie along the coast, separated from the interior by high plateaus and mountain ranges, which include Morocco's highest peak, Toubkal, at 13,671 feet (4,167 meters). Lower desert lands lie to the east and south. Most rivers and lakes are seasonal. During dry summers they contain hardly any water. The fine, rich soil in riverbeds and lake bottoms is used for growing crops in dry summers. Earthquakes are major natural hazards.

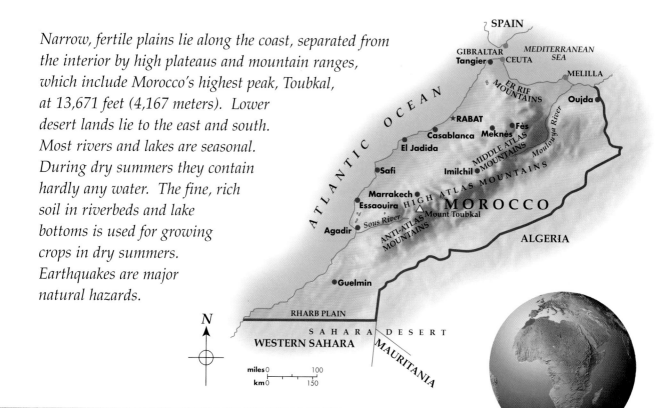

Sure-footed mules have been used for centuries to carry people and farm produce along steep, narrow mountain paths in Morocco's High Atlas Mountains.

CLIMATE

Morocco has a generally mild climate. Rainfall is most plentiful in the north and decreases toward the south. A dry season extends from April to October, when a hot, dry wind blows from the Sahara Desert. In winter the high mountains receive heavy falls of snow.

	Rabat	Marrakech
Average January temperature:	54°F (12°C)	52°F (11°C)
Average July temperature:	74°F (23°C)	85°F (29°C)
Average annual precipitation:	35 in. (89 cm)	10 in. (25 cm)

Berbers and Muslims

Hunter-gatherers lived in Morocco (muh-RAH-koe) from about twenty thousand years ago. The Berber (BUHR-buhr) people have lived there since before 2000 B.C.E. as hunters, herders, and farmers. For most of its history, Morocco has not been a united country; instead the Berbers have ruled small, independent states. In 105 B.C.E. Romans invaded the region. The lands between Tangier (tan-JIR) and Rabat (ruh-BAHT) became a province of the Roman Empire, called Mauretania Tingitana, but the Berbers kept control of the mountain regions of Morocco and the desert south.

In 429 C.E. armies of Vandals from eastern Europe ended Roman power, and the Berbers ruled Morocco once again. Then, between 683 and 705, the first of many groups of Muslim soldiers and farmers arrived from Arabia and the Middle East. Some settled in Morocco; others traveled through it on their way to conquer southern Spain. The Berbers rebelled against rule by these Muslim invaders, but they were unable to halt the growth of independent Muslim kingdoms along the north African coast.

Muslim settlers continued to arrive in Morocco until the eleventh century, but the Berbers remained in the majority. During this era most Berber people converted to Islam, though they kept many of their own customs and traditions, as well as their language and their political independence.

From about 1060 Morocco was ruled by Berber Muslim dynasties: the Almoravids, the Almohads, and the Merenids. Under

FACTS AND FIGURES

Official name: Al-Mamlakah al-Maghribiyah (Kingdom of the West)

Status: Independent state

Capital: Rabat

Major towns: Casablanca, Tangier, Marrakech, Fès, Meknès

Area: 172,413 square miles (446,550 square kilometers)

Population: 28,200,000

Population density: 164 per square mile (63 per square kilometer)

Peoples: A majority of the population are of mixed Arab-Berber ancestry; about one-third of the population identify themselves as Berber

Official language: Arabic

Currency: Dirham

National days: Feast of the Throne (March 3); Anniversary of the Green March (November 6); Independence Day (November 18)

Country's name: Al-Maghrib is Arabic for "the West." Morocco is from the old European name Moors, which referred to people of mixed Arab-Berber ancestry.

their leadership Morocco was unified for the first time.

During the fifteenth and sixteenth centuries, rulers of Spain and Portugal attacked Morocco and conquered the cities of Agadir (ah-gah-DIR), Ceuta (THAE-oo-tah), and Tangier. These attacks halted after the Moroccans defeated the Portuguese in battle in 1578.

In 1666, after a civil war between rival Moroccan families, the Alawite dynasty

Time line:	Stone Age hunters and gatherers in Morocco	Berber hunters, herders, and farmers settle in northern Africa	Romans rule northern Africa until Vandals invade	Muslim Arabs arrive
	18,000 B.C.E.	before 2000 B.C.E.	105 B.C.E.–429 C.E.	683–1000s C.E.

Fine plasterwork and a beautiful tiled floor decorate the Qarawiyin Mosque in Fès. Founded in 859 C.E., it is one of the oldest Muslim buildings in northern Africa.

European Claims

During the early nineteenth century, European nations began to compete for control of northern Africa. In 1830 France invaded Algeria and set its sights on Morocco. Sultan Moulay al-Hassan, who ruled from 1873 to 1894, tried to keep out Europeans but was not completely successful, and many European businesses began to operate in Morocco. The sultan also introduced economic, administrative, and military reforms designed to strengthen the country and guard against foreign takeovers.

However, pressure from Europe continued. In 1884 Spain claimed the right to "protect" lands along the Moroccan coast. Ten years later the French invaded but were forced to retreat. In the early 1900s France again tried to win control of Morocco by peaceful negotiations. In 1912 all the strongest European powers agreed that most of Morocco should become a protectorate of France, with Spain controlling parts of the northern coast. Morocco was powerless to resist.

came to power. At first it controlled only the area around Fès, but after ruthless campaigns by Sultan Ismail al-Hasani (1672–1727), it gradually extended its rule. Ismail al-Hasani's descendants still rule Morocco today.

After 1912 many French colonists arrived to set up vineyards and farms. The first French resident-general, Louis Lyautey,

Under the Almoravids, Morocco becomes a united kingdom	Moroccans defeat Portuguese	Alawite dynasty comes to power	Europeans try to take over Morocco
ca. 1060	1578	1666	1830–1912

represented the interests of the French government, leading a campaign to extend French control into the most remote mountain areas. From 1921 to 1926 there was bitter fighting as Berber troops, led by Abd-el-Krim, fought unsuccessfully to keep the Spanish and French out of their lands. In 1923, after further European negotiations, the strategically important city of Tangier, which controlled the Strait of Gibraltar, was made an international zone, without Moroccan consent.

Independence and Royal Rule

In 1944 the Moroccan Independence Party was formed. Its supporters, backed by Sultan Muhammad V, boycotted French goods and carried out terrorist attacks. As a punishment, he was exiled from Morocco in 1953, which led to protests from the international community. In 1955 the sultan returned home to a great welcome. France realized that it could not keep control of Morocco, except by obviously unjust force, and so in 1956, Morocco's independence was declared. Spain also agreed to hand over control of the northern region, except for Ceuta, Melilla (muh-LEE-lyah), and a cluster of small offshore islands. Morocco and Spain are still in dispute over this territory today (see CEUTA AND MELILLA).

In 1961 Sultan Muhammad V died; his son became King Hassan II. In 1971 republicans, who wanted a more modern and democratic system of government, attempted a coup, but it failed. Responding to their protests, the king introduced a new constitution in 1972, based on free elections rather than direct royal rule. But most of its reforms were suspended after another attempted coup, and the king remained in charge.

During the 1970s and 1980s, King Hassan's popularity increased as a result of his plans to win more territory for Morocco. In 1975 he led civilians on a march to seize control of disputed land in neighboring Western Sahara from Spain (see WESTERN SAHARA). In 1979 he agreed to a treaty with Mauritania, settling boundary disputes, and in 1984 he signed a treaty to end a quarrel with Libya, which had been backing Western Sahara rebels, who wanted independence from Morocco and Spain.

However, droughts and falling profits from exports during the 1980s led to economic problems. Food prices rose, and people rioted for bread. King Hassan turned to wealthy countries for help, especially the United States. They advised strict economic reforms, which reduced the wages of many ordinary people. Throughout the early 1990s there were strikes and protests against low earnings and poor social conditions and demands for government reform. In the 1993 elections, supporters of King Hassan gained a small overall majority, but the Bloc Démocratique coalition, which opposed him, won a large share of the vote. Protesters claimed that the king kept hold of power through human rights abuses and by taking political prisoners. International humanitarian organizations agreed with many of their claims. King Hassan II died in 1999, and his son, Muhammad VI,

Morocco becomes a protectorate of France; Spain controls part of northern coast	Unsuccessful war against Spanish and French	Start of campaign for Moroccan independence	Morocco becomes independent
1912	1921–1926	1944	1956

Shopkeepers receive a customer in the town of Essaouira (eh-sah-WEE-rah). The remains of many Arab, Berber, French, and Portuguese buildings still stand there.

assumed power. He pledged to continue his father's policies and constitution.

Today, thanks to help from international aid organizations, Morocco's economy has improved, but unemployment and foreign debts are still high. Social problems have grown in crowded big-city slums. There is an increasing level of Muslim fundamentalist activity, but this is not a serious threat to stability. Disputes continue with Spain and Western Sahara over Moroccan boundaries, and many still call for an end to royal rule. However, compared with many other African nations, Morocco is peaceful and prosperous, with good health care and opportunities for education.

A Mix of Berbers and Arabs

Most people in Morocco are of mixed ancestry. They are descended from Berbers, the original inhabitants of northern Africa; from the Arab soldiers and settlers who arrived in northern Africa from the Middle East during the seventh to the eleventh centuries; and from Muslims of mixed Arab, Berber, and Spanish descent, driven out of Spain by Christian rulers after 1492.

Today, Moroccans speak Arabic or one of the Berber languages. In big cities and in farmland close to the northern coast, most

Hassan II becomes king	King Hassan leads march to seize Western Sahara	Economic problems	Demands for economic and political reform; protests against human rights abuses	Hassan II dies
1961	**1975**	**1980s**	**1990s**	**1999**

Carrying a basket of herbs, this Berber girl returns to her village in the Atlas Mountains. Most Berbers live in the countryside, as they have done for more than four thousand years.

language they speak. The Zenatiya (zeh-NAHT-yah) live in the Er Rif Mountains of the north; the Tamazight (TAH-muh-zite) dwell in the central High and Middle Atlas mountain regions; the Tashelheyt (teh-SHEHL-aet) live in the Anti-Atlas Mountains, the Sous Valley, and desert oasis towns, all in the far south. Within each region the Berbers are organized into smaller clans or tribes. Councils of senior men (usually heads of families) run villages and country districts. They administer laws, which regulate livestock, housing, and all kinds of minor crimes that might disrupt the community.

people speak Arabic. They are, therefore, often known as Arabs. They work in modern offices, stores, and factories, in the mining and construction industries, or on large, irrigated farms producing fruit and vegetables for export, mostly to Europe. Many are employed in the tourist industry, running hotels and restaurants, driving coaches, or acting as tour guides and interpreters.

Further inland, in Morocco's mountain and desert regions, most people speak a Berber language as their native tongue and follow long-established Berber customs. These Berbers are divided into three different groups, according to the local

Stories and Songs

Popular musicians and storytellers, known as heddaoua *(heh-DAH-wah), strengthen the Berbers' sense of identity. They travel from one village to another, reciting poetry and folktales and playing music. Until recently, Berber history and literature has not been written down but has been preserved and passed by word of mouth among families and by storytellers. Today, television is replacing traditional entertainments in many Berber villages, but Berber cultural associations are working hard to preserve and promote their peoples' language and culture.*

Although men are the leaders of village life, older women, especially mothers of married sons, can be powerful within Berber households. Unlike many other Muslim women, Berber wives and daughters have considerable freedom to appear in public and to run farms and businesses alongside men. They dress modestly in long, loose clothes, but they do not veil their faces and they rarely cover their heads. As well as laboring in the fields, they often work as market traders, selling fruits and vegetables produced on their family farms. At festivals and family celebrations, they take part in communal dances alongside men, something that other Muslim women would never do.

Many Berbers live as farmers, raising sheep and goats and growing olive trees and grain, mostly wheat. In the desert they grow fruit and date palms at oases. In scenic tourist areas, especially in the mountains, they work in hotels and as guides. In country areas many Berber families live in *ksour* (KSOOR), or fortified villages, which often have an *agadir* (AH-guh-deer), or a communal granary, within their walls. Traditionally Berber villages were clustered around a *kasbah* (KAJ-bah), the house of the locally powerful clan leader. Most Berber houses and farms are still built of pounded earth and sun-baked clay bricks. They have narrow slit windows for coolness and tall, tapering towers.

Changing Lives

In many ways Morocco seems to be a very modern country, with big cities, high-rise buildings, hotels, movie theaters, airports, good roads, and up-to-date technology. About half the population lives in modern, Western-style houses in cities and towns. In the northern region both men and women wear Western-style clothes and follow European or American fashions. Women work in professional jobs such as teaching and medicine. By law they have equal access with men to education and civil rights.

In recent years society has been changing fast, as many families leave village homelands to seek work in cities and towns. There, they rent apartments and shop in supermarkets rather than build

Wearing magnificent amber and silver jewelry, this young Berber woman attends the annual marriage fair at Imilchil in the Atlas Mountains, hoping to find a husband.

Two men in traditional dress deep in discussion in the street. Moroccan men also gather in cafés and restaurants to talk, read, or enjoy games of checkers, backgammon, and chess.

their own houses and grow their own food, as their ancestors would have done. They no longer belong to close-knit village communities where their behavior was shaped by long established customs.

However, many Moroccan social customs are still conservative. In line with Muslim values, men play the leading role in public; outside their homes, women do not socialize with men, except for members of their families. Public displays of affection between men and women are frowned on, and neither men nor women wear tight, short, or revealing clothes.

Language and Religion

Arabic is the official language of Morocco, although many Moroccan people speak a Berber language and sometimes French or

Spanish as well. French is spoken in cosmopolitan cities like Casablanca (kah-suh-BLAHNG-kuh) and Tangier. For writing, Moroccans use Modern Standard Arabic, written in a basic Arabic script that can be read in all Arabic-speaking lands. All Moroccans speak their own version of the Arabic language, though, which can be difficult for non-Moroccans to understand. There are over three hundred local dialects of the Berber language, written in an ancient script, and many Berber people speak Arabic as a second language.

More than 90 percent of Moroccans are Muslim. In the past in Berber areas, the faith of Islam has sometimes mingled with the remains of earlier, non-Muslim beliefs. These beliefs centered on ancient holy places inhabited by powerful, invisible

A desert nomad holds a wooden board on which texts from the Koran (the holy book of Islam) are written. Islam arrived in northern Africa more than one thousand years ago.

spirits. Today many Berbers honor the spirits of dead Muslim religious leaders and make pilgrimages to their tombs.

Throughout Morocco several ancient superstitions still survive. For example, many people still believe in the power of the Evil Eye, a force stirred up by hatred or envy. They decorate their buildings with patterns of handprints to push the Evil Eye away and to protect their household from harm.

Money for Education and Health Care

Morocco has a long tradition of excellence in education. The Islamic University of Qarawiyin (founded 859 C.E.) is one of the most famous and prestigious universities in the Muslim world. The newer Muhammad V University (founded 1957) also has a good reputation. There are nine other universities, attended by over 200,000 students. In recent years the government of Morocco has been committed to improving education and has spent almost a quarter of its budget on schools and colleges.

Schooling is free and compulsory for boys and girls ages seven to thirteen, and over three-quarters of eligible pupils attend. In the past, however, fewer opportunities for primary education existed, which explains why many Moroccan adults today (about four out of every ten men and six out of every ten women) still cannot read and write.

Today Moroccan children receive a good basic education. When this girl grows up, she will also have the opportunity to train for a professional career.

Compared with many other African countries, health care facilities in Morocco are good. Most people live within reach of a doctor or trained nurse. Today the average man can expect to reach the age of sixty-six, and women can live to an average age of seventy-one, although differences in health care between rich and poor people and between country districts and towns remain. In remote rural areas and among poor people, malaria, typhoid, tuberculosis, trachoma (a bacterial eye disease), and diseases caused by polluted drinking water still cause suffering and early death.

A fishing boat leaves the harbor at El Jadida (EL JAW-dee-duh), an important sardine-fishing port on the Atlantic coast. Fish is exported to many parts of the world.

A Mixed Economy

Like Moroccan society, the Moroccan economy is a mixture of old and new. About half the population works in agriculture, but industry (mining and manufacturing), together with tourism, produces more wealth. About one person in eight is unemployed, and there is a growing gap between a small, rich minority and the large majority, who are poorer.

Moroccan farming varies from region to region. Along the Atlantic coast and on the Rharb Plain, farms are large and mechanized. Fields and orchards are often irrigated.

Farmers here grow wheat, barley, citrus fruits, vegetables, and grapes. Fruits and vegetables, which ripen early in Morocco's warm spring sunshine, are exported to Europe. In the mountains, farmers grow olives and raise sheep and cattle. Forests cover about 20 percent of the mountain lands; cork (used for bottle stoppers and floor coverings) and timber are harvested for export. Busy fishing ports line the Atlantic and Mediterranean coasts.

Morocco has rich mineral reserves; its deserts and mountains contain almost 75 percent of the world's phosphate (a rock that is crushed to make fertilizer). The country also has valuable deposits of copper, rock salt, iron ore, coal, lead, manganese, and zinc. An industrial region

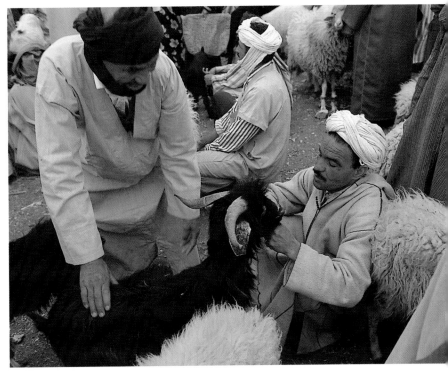

Shepherds and their sheep at Guelmim (gool-MEEM), a cattle-market town in southern Morocco, on the edge of the Sahara. Camels and goats are also sold here.

flourishes around the cities of Casablanca and Rabat; factories there produce plastics, textiles, leather goods, glassware, furniture, electrical equipment, and machine tools. They also make processed foods.

In spite of these industries, Morocco is not a wealthy country. It cannot grow enough to feed its fast-increasing population and has to import food, petroleum, and machinery. It relies on money sent home from Moroccans working abroad (mainly in southern Europe), on earnings from tourism, and on overseas aid to survive.

Flavorful Food

Moroccan food is full of flavor. The most popular dish is couscous, tiny pellets of semolina—coarsely ground wheat flour—steamed and topped with meat or vegetable sauce. *Harira* (huh-REER-uh), lentil soup with hot chili peppers, is another favorite. For celebrations, Moroccan cooks prepare *tajines* (tuh-ZHINZ), slow-cooked meat stews with spices and dried fruits, or *pastilla* (PAHST-lah), a rich pigeon pie flavored with sugar and nuts. Seafood is available in coastal towns. For dessert, Moroccans eat European-style pastries, such as doughnuts, and fresh local fruit, especially oranges, mandarin oranges, bananas, grapes, dates, and watermelons. Hot, sweet, milkless tea, flavored with mint, is the most popular drink, together with strong black coffee. Red wine is produced for export and, although many Muslims do not approve, for local consumption.

Artistic Heritage

Morocco's rich artistic heritage has been proudly preserved. Many fine ancient Muslim buildings, especially mosques and

Meat and Couscous

You will need:
- *1 20-ounce (567-gram) can of cooked chickpeas*
- *1½ pounds (680 grams) of lamb shank*
- *2 teaspoons (10 grams) salt*
- *2 teaspoons (10 grams) black pepper*
- *1 teaspoon (5 grams) ground ginger*
- *¼ teaspoon (1.25 grams) turmeric*
- *1 pinch of cayenne pepper*
- *3 quartered medium onions*
- *1 cup (250 grams) butter*
- *1 large Spanish onion, thinly sliced*
- *½ cup (125 grams) raisins*
- *2 cups (500 grams) couscous*

Place the lamb, salt, pepper, spices, onions, and half the butter in a large, heavy saucepan. Melt the butter over low heat, swirling the pan to mix the ingredients. Cover with 2½ quarts (2.4 liters) water and bring to boil. Simmer for ninety minutes.

Carefully remove the lamb bone from the pan and cut the meat into bite-sized pieces. Return meat to broth along with Spanish onion, chickpeas, and raisins. Simmer for twenty minutes.

Put the couscous in a bowl, add 2 quarts (1.9 liters) freshly boiled water, and leave it to stand for five minutes. When the couscous has absorbed all the water, fluff it up with a fork and stir in remaining butter. Serve with the spiced meat and chickpeas on top. Sprinkle a few drops of a hot-pepper sauce over the dish if desired.

This quantity serves six people.

Moroccan Music

Settlers and invaders from many lands have come to live in Morocco, and many of their musical styles have survived, sometimes blending together, sometimes staying apart. Moroccan music is widely admired in northern Africa and many other lands. Some players still perform traditional Berber dances and songs on Berber instruments such as the amzhad (uhm-ZHAHD), a goatskin-covered violin, and bendir (behn-DEER), which is a handheld drum, or on typical northern African instruments such as the ghalta (GAHL-tah), or oboe, qaraqib (kuh-ruh-KEEB), or castanets, and lira (LIH-rah), or flute. Other players perform nawba (NAW-buh), collections of songs and instrumental pieces that originated over a thousand years ago in Muslim Spain. A few performers, such as Hassan Erraji, the famous oud (OOD), or lute, player, experiment by blending Arabic musical styles with instruments and themes from modern Western music.

madrasas (muh-DRAH-suhs), or Islamic colleges, still stand, along with fascinating old towns, with strong walls and gates, narrow, twisting streets, fine courtyard houses, and covered marketplaces. Arts and crafts include beautiful leather work, brightly

(above) Silver jewelry made by Berber artisans. Large, dramatic pieces are the most popular.

(left) Brightly patterned pottery is a specialty of Moroccan towns such as Safi and Fès.

patterned pottery and ceramic tiles, delicately woven woolen carpets and rugs, elaborate silver jewelry, and decorative objects, such as bowls and little statues, skillfully made from fossils and semiprecious stones found in the deserts and mountains.

MOZAMBIQUE

M ozambique occupies the coast of southeastern Africa, between Tanzania and South Africa.

Coral reefs, islands, lagoons, and mangroves fringe Mozambique's long coast. Three great rivers cross the coastal plain: the Limpopo, the Save, and the Zambezi. The capital, Maputo, has one of the best natural harbors in Africa.

Inland, Mozambique rises to a plateau and highlands. The country's highest point is Mount Binga on the Zimbabwe border, which is 7,992 feet (2,436 meters) above sea level.

CLIMATE

Mozambique has a humid, tropical climate. Its wet season lasts from November to March. The highlands receive the most rainfall. A dry season usually lingers between April and October, but on the southern coastal plains it often extends to form prolonged droughts.

	Maputo	**Beira**
Average January temperature:	78°F (26°C)	82°F (28°C)
Average July temperature:	65°F (18°C)	69°F (21°C)
Average annual precipitation:	30 in. (76 cm)	60 in. (152 cm)

Fishermen carry their catch from the boat on a pole at a beach near Quelimane (kuh-lee-MAW-nuh). Fish and prawns from the Indian Ocean are an important source of food in a hungry country.

A Land of Traders

Humans have lived in the Mozambique (moe-zahm-BEEK) region as hunters and gatherers for many thousands of years. Bantu-speaking peoples from the north and west (see CAMEROON) began arriving in the region nearly two thousand years ago, gradually displacing the hunter-gatherers. The Bantu were skilled ironworkers. They forged weapons and tools for farming.

The next arrivals, sometime between 800 and 900 C.E., were Arab merchants, who

traded across the Indian Ocean. Some settled along the coast, bringing the religion of Islam to the region and intermarrying with local Bantu-speaking coastal people. From this mix emerged the Swahili (swah-HEE-lee) people, who built towns such as Sofala (probably modern Beira) in the 1200s and controlled the coastal trade. The Swahili, dealing in ivory and gold, traded with the African peoples occupying the Zambezi (zam-BEE-zee) Valley.

In the 1480s the Zambezi Valley came under the rule of a large Bantu-speaking empire known as the Maravi Confederacy, whose center was in what is now Malawi (see MALAWI). By 1650 the Maravi Confederacy stretched from the northern bank of the Zambezi River to the east coast around Moçambique Island and dominated the ivory trade of the region.

Under the Portuguese

During the early sixteenth century, the Portuguese arrived on the coast, lured by reports of the rich gold trade with the African interior. They also wanted to set up supply posts for their voyages to Asia. They soon clashed with the Swahili. The Portuguese sacked rich Swahili towns. They demolished mosques and used coral rock from the mosques to build fortresses. Like the Swahili, these Europeans traded profitably with the Maravi Confederacy.

The Portuguese attempted to establish a monopoly over the ivory trade in the lower Zambezi Valley. Their violence provoked the local people they displaced into

---

FACTS AND FIGURES

Official name: República de Moçambique

Status: Independent state

Capital: Maputo

Major towns: Beira, Nampula, Nacala, Quelimane

Area: 297,846 square miles (771,421 square kilometers)

Population: 19,100,000

Population density: 64 per square mile (25 per square kilometer)

Peoples: 38 percent Makua-Lomwe; 24 percent Tsonga; 12 percent Maravi peoples; 6 percent Shona; 3 percent Yao; 16 percent other Bantu-speaking groups; 1 percent European, Asian, and mixed descent

Official language: Portuguese

Currency: Metical

National days: Heroes' Day (February 3); Independence Day (June 25)

Country's name: The name comes from Moçambique Island.

Time line:	Evidence of hunter-gatherers living in Mozambique	Bantu peoples in control of region	Arabs settle on northern coast	Swahili settlement reaches Sofala
	ca. 2000 B.C.E.	ca. 200 C.E.	800s	1200s

Ceramic tiles, terra-cotta roofs, and white walls in the capital, Maputo, are reminders of the Portuguese. This building is named after the Algarve, a region of Portugal.

forming an army and resisting the Portuguese in the 1580s.

From the 1630s the Portuguese moved inland south of the Zambezi River toward the Zimbabwe plateau to try to take control of the gold trade there. The region and the trade were controlled by the Shona (SHOE-nah) people of the Mwene Mutapa state, located on the Zambezi escarpment in what is now Zimbabwe (see ZIMBABWE). Portuguese attempts to control gold mining, using forced labor and much violence, provoked Shona resistance. Soldiers of the Rozvi Empire, also on the Zimbabwe plateau, eventually drove the Portuguese back down into the Zambezi Valley.

During the 1700s and 1800s, some Portuguese traders settled in the Zambezi Valley. These men, known as *prazeros* (prah-

ZAE-roz), broke away from Portuguese control, married African women, and set themselves up as local chiefs, with armies of captive slaves. The prazeros ruled huge estates and treated the local Africans as their subjects. The African peoples and the prazeros of Mozambique continued to resist Portuguese rule, and the colonists were confined to the coast and the lower Zambezi Valley until the end of the nineteenth century. A series of treaties between Portugal and Germany and Portugal and Great Britain between 1885 and 1890 established the boundaries of the colony of Portuguese East Africa, as Mozambique was called.

In the 1930s the Portuguese drove peasant farmers off their land and set up plantations of rice and cotton. These crops were grown as cash crops for export. The plantations employed forced labor under brutal conditions. Local agriculture was abandoned, resulting in famine. More and more workers fled abroad rather than endure conditions close to slavery.

Frelimo and Renamo

In 1962, as independence movements were sweeping across the African continent, a number of small rebel groups allied to form a liberation movement called Frelimo; its name stood for Frente de Libertaçao de Moçambique (Mozambique Liberation Front). Within two years Frelimo had

Maravi Confederacy expands its rule in the region	Coast ruled by Portuguese; slave trade develops	Portuguese try to move inland but are driven back	Portuguese rule coast; Lower Zambezi Valley under control of Afro-Portuguese chiefdoms	Region becomes the colony of Portuguese East Africa
1480s–1650	1500s	1600s	1700s–1800s	1890

launched a full-scale guerrilla war against the Portuguese. In 1974 a revolution in Portugal brought democracy to that country, and by the end of that year Frelimo controlled most of rural Mozambique. The new Portuguese government announced its withdrawal from colonial rule in Africa and handed over power to Frelimo in 1975. Portuguese settlers soon fled from Mozambique.

When Mozambique became independent in 1975, its president was Frelimo leader Samora Machel. The government, supported by the communist Soviet Union, developed a one-party, socialist state in which peasants, workers, and women all gained a voice for the first time.

In 1977 the security forces of neighboring Rhodesia (now Zimbabwe), then a colony controlled by whites (see ZIMBABWE), set up Renamo, an antigovernment guerrilla group of Mozambicans. Renamo (which stands for Resistência Nacional Moçambicana, or the Mozambique National Resistance) attacked both the training camps of Zimbabwean independence fighters and the roads and rail links in Mozambique. After Zimbabwe gained independence in 1980, Renamo was funded by the United States and South Africa. The United States opposed Mozambique's links with the Soviet Union, and the white, racist government then ruling South Africa feared military bases being set up in Mozambique by its own chief opponent, the African National Congress.

The disastrous war that followed lasted fifteen years, causing slaughter and starvation. It left a devastated land strewn with deadly landmines. The early 1980s saw terrible droughts and floods as well as severe economic problems caused by the war.

In 1990 the constitution was changed to make Mozambique a multiparty state. Frelimo gave up its socialist program and reached a peace settlement with Renamo in 1992. About a million people died during the fighting, and many more were orphaned or maimed. Renamo, heavily funded by the United States, reestablished itself as a political party. However, Frelimo, under Joaquim Chissano, still won the 1994 elections, which were recognized internationally as free and fair.

Mozambicans were at last able to begin rebuilding their country under peaceful conditions. Through the 1990s Mozambique achieved very high rates of economic growth, prospects for the future looked bright, and Chissano and Frelimo were re-elected to government in December 1999. In February 2000, however, Mozambique was devastated by the heaviest floods in living memory. Roads and bridges were destroyed and hundreds of thousands were left homeless as whole villages were swept away in the floodwaters. Development was set back at least a decade and Mozambique will now need huge and sustained inputs of foreign aid for reconstruction.

Rebuilding Mozambique

Many of Mozambique's problems date from the days of colonial rule. Few Africans had been educated. Hardly any could read or

Peasant farmers evicted; plantations set up	Frelimo starts war of independence	Mozambique becomes independent	Renamo founded to resist government	Peace accord with Renamo ends civil war	Frelimo wins elections	Disasterous floods
1930s	1964	1975	1977	1992	1994	2000

This starving child is being weighed by health workers. After the terrors of civil war, saving lives through medical help and adequate nutrition is a priority.

born, 176 will die before they reach their fifth birthday. Males can expect to live only until age forty-five, and females to age forty-eight.

Eight out of ten workers in Mozambique live off the land. In the north they are farmers, raising crops by methods in which plots of land are cleared, cultivated, and then allowed to grow over while another plot is cleared. Most farmers grow just enough corn, cassava, sorghum, and bananas for their own needs or the local market. Cash crops are grown too, including sisal (a fibrous plant used to make twine), sugarcane, cotton, tea, cashews, and rice. Coconut groves are found in coastal areas. Cattle are raised in the south, although there have been long-standing problems with tsetse flies, which cause diseases among the cattle as well as sleeping sickness in humans.

Much of the plateau region is forested and forestry is important to the economy. Fishing is one of the most

write. The war then interrupted Frelimo's education plans, so that few children received the seven years of schooling that they were supposed to. Despite this, 64 percent of men and 37 percent of women can now read and write. This difference in numbers reflects traditional male-female roles and should change, since Frelimo is committed to improving the position of women in society.

Mozambique's problems are extreme. There is only one doctor per 36,225 members of the population. Tuberculosis, pneumonia, and gastric diseases are common. Out of every thousand children

A worker looks out over the oil terminal at Beira. This major port is linked by railroad with Zimbabwe, Zambia, Malawi, and the Democratic Republic of Congo.

important export industries, with shrimps and lobsters caught in the Indian Ocean.

The food most people eat is very similar to that in many other African countries. The most common food is cornmeal, boiled and pressed into a ball of dough. This may be served with freshwater fish caught from the country's many rivers and streams or with seafood, vegetables, or meat.

Mozambique has reserves of coal, bauxite, graphite, and salt. Other mineral resources are still to be developed, including iron ore, gold, natural gas, and precious stones. Since the 1970s the Zambezi River has been dammed to form a lake at the Cabora Bassa (kaw-BAWR-uh BAW-suh) gorge. This dam is one of Africa's biggest hydroelectric projects, producing electricity for sale mostly to South Africa. The lake supplies water for crop irrigation.

People and Languages

Two-thirds of Mozambique's people live in the country. Traditional villages consist of round homes built of dried mud and timber, with thatched roofs. The towns include modern buildings and offices and run-down housing with poor utility services. Many country people come to Maputo (mah-POO-toe), the capital, in a vain search for work.

The official language of Mozambique is Portuguese, but very few people speak it outside the cities. Thirty-three other languages can be heard. Swahili, the common language of eastern Africa (see KENYA), is widely spoken on the coast. English is now taught in schools and is likely to replace Portuguese as the country's language of international communication.

Probably over half the population follow African religions. These include beliefs in spirits and in a force present in all aspects of

When the Buffalo Died

For hundreds of years stories were passed on from one generation to another by word of mouth. This sad tale was told by the Ronga (RAWN-gah) people who live south of Maputo. Its message is that individuals need to follow the customs of the tribe and obey the advice of their elders.

Once upon a time there was a young man whose parents tried to arrange a marriage for him. The young man went off wandering to distant lands, where he found the young woman he desired and took her home.

The bride's family wanted to send many servants with her. She insisted on taking the tribe's magical buffalo instead, for it was said to be able to do any kind of work. The young man and his bride were welcomed to his home. The buffalo hid away in the forest but secretly did all her hard work. However, the buffalo soon began to steal crops from the fields. One day the young man tracked down the buffalo and killed it.

The young woman had no choice but to return to her village, pretending to be ill. She sang the song of the buffalo's death, and all her people wept, for if the buffalo died, they would all have to die. The magical life source of the tribe had been broken.

nature and in honoring the spirits of one's ancestors. Christianity arrived with the Portuguese, and today nearly one-third of the population are Christian. The majority of these are Roman Catholics, living in the southern half of the country. The remainder of the population are mostly Muslims, living in the north. Hindu temples can be seen in the small Indian communities.

The north-south divide extends beyond religion, with the Zambezi River forming

Roman Catholics take part in Sunday Mass near Tete (TAE-tuh) in the central region. Portuguese missionaries first brought Christianity to Mozambique.

Tanzania. About 60 percent of the Makua-Lomwe hold African religious beliefs. People tie cloths to trees as offerings to the spirit world and often wear amulets, or charms, on their wrists or upper arms. The remainder of the Makua-Lomwe are usually Muslim or Christian.

The Tsonga (TSAWN-gah) make up about 24 percent of the total population. Many of them work in South Africa. Tsonga villages are scattered on the southern coastal plain. While most Tsonga are Christian, African beliefs, with an emphasis on ancestor worship, are still common. Illness or misfortune are believed to be the result of breaking a taboo, failing to honor one's ancestors correctly, or sorcery. Tsonga men often marry more than one woman, and their

something of a cultural divide as well as a geographical one. For example, north of the Zambezi, descent is traced on the mother's side, in the south on the father's.

However, day-to-day life for most people in Mozambique is much the same. Western dress is widespread, with the women favoring brightly colored cotton wraps and head scarves.

The most numerous ethnic group in Mozambique is referred to as Makua-Lomwe (MAHK-wa-LOEM-wae). This is really a family of related peoples who together may account for 38 percent or more of the total population. Their territory covers the northern and central regions and extends across into Malawi and

People who fall ill may make herbal medicines from ingredients such as these for sale at a market stall. Some herbal remedies are undoubtedly good for the patient, while others may be of psychological benefit.

Marika to Marribenta

Mozambique has always been a land of music, with the soulful fado (FAH-thoo) folk songs of the Portuguese contrasting with the gentle marika *(muh-REE-kuh) folk music of the African countryside. The Chopi played—and still play, often in orchestras—xylophones called* timbila *(tihm-BEE-lah). The Makonde made wooden flutes, called* lupembe *(loo-PEHM-bee). In Maputo an urban version of marika developed, called* marribenta *(mah-ree-BEHN-tah). This was dance music, using guitars, trumpets, saxophones, drums, and other percussion. It became the music associated with the Frelimo years and reached an international audience. Marribenta remains popular today.*

livestock is shared among the various wives' families.

Other large groups include the Sena (SAE-nah) of the northwest and the lower Zambezi. The Shona (SHOE-nah) group live near the border with Zimbabwe (see ZIMBABWE). The Chewa (CHEE-wah) and Nyanja (NYAHN-jah) claim descent from the peoples of the Maravi Confederacy, while the Yao (YAH-oe)—living in the north-central area south of Lake Malawi— once traded slaves between Malawi and the coast (see MALAWI). The Makonde (muh-KOEN-dee) straddle the Tanzanian border (see TANZANIA), and the Chopi (SHOE-pee) live on the southern coast north of the Limpopo. There are numerous smaller Bantu-speaking groups, and in the coastal cities live small communities of Asians of Indian and Chinese descent and Europeans.

Children put on costumes and make up a dance on the streets of Maputo. Hopefully they will enjoy a better life than the children of the war years.

369

NAMIBIA

Namibia lies on the coast of southwestern Africa.

The Namib Desert along the Atlantic coast is barren land, marked in some areas by enormous sand dunes. Down the middle of the country runs a plateau, reaching heights of 4,000 feet (1,200 meters). Here grasses, shrubs, and small trees grow. In the southeastern Kalahari Desert grow grasses and thornbushes. In the north, where rainfall is higher and the rivers flood, are fertile land and taller trees.

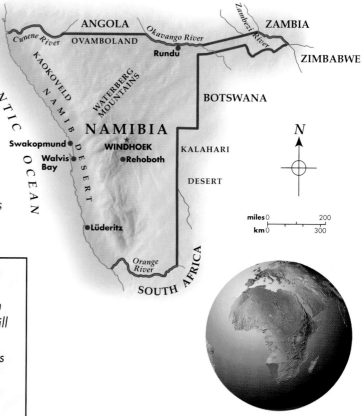

CLIMATE

In the Namib Desert, summer temperatures can be as high as 110°F (43°C), but in winter it will plunge to below freezing. Fog is common on the coast. On the central plateau the climate is more moderate.

Average January temperature: *75°F (24°C)*

Average July temperature: *55°F (13°C)*

Average annual precipitation: *10 in. (25 cm)*

This child wears the leather dress of the Himba people. The Himba live in Namibia's northwestern Kaokoveld, looking after their cattle and goats.

A Land of Conflict and Oppression

The earliest inhabitants of southern Africa were the San (SAHN), who were already hunting animals and gathering wild food about twenty thousand years ago. From about 300 B.C.E., Nama (NAH-mah), or Khoi-Khoi (KOY-koy), people moved in from the area of present-day Botswana, pushing the San toward the Namib Desert. The Nama too were hunter-gatherers, but they also kept domestic animals.

FACTS AND FIGURES

Official name: *Republic of Namibia*

Status: *Independent state*

Capital: *Windhoek*

Major towns: *Swakopmund, Rundu, Rehoboth*

Area: *318,321 square miles (824,451 square kilometers)*

Population: *1,600,000*

Population density: *5 per square mile (2 per square kilometer)*

Peoples: *About 85 percent Bantu-speakers, including Ovambo (50 percent), Kavango (9 percent), Herero (8 percent), and Himba, and Khoisan-speakers, including Damara (8 percent), Nama, and San; 10 percent of mixed descent, primarily Afrikaner-Khoi-Khoi; 5 percent Europeans, including Afrikaner and German*

Official language: *English*

Currency: *Namibian dollar*

National days: *Independence Day (March 21); Cassinga Day (May 4); Heroes Day (August 26)*

Country's name: *In 1966 the United Nations named the country after the Namib Desert. Namib is a Khoi-Khoi word meaning "desert."*

Bantu-speaking people from central Africa began moving into Namibia (nuh-MIH-bee-uh) during the 1400s C.E. In the coastal region and the northwestern Kaokoveld (KAW-koe-felt), the Herero (heh-REH-roe), a Bantu-speaking people, settled with their herds of cattle. By the eighteenth century they were in central Namibia, where the grazing was good.

Ovambo (oe-VAHM-boe) farmers from present-day Zambia settled in the fertile lands of the north, while the Damara (duh-MAH-rah) people colonized the central highlands. During the 1800s the Nama and the Herero battled frequently over control of the grazing lands of the central highlands. The Oorlams (OOR-lahms), a mixed-race people of mostly Khoi-Khoi with some European ancestry, also moved into the area from the south.

The Nama-Herero wars alarmed British traders and German missionaries, who had arrived in the region during the 1830s and 1840s. Both groups asked their homelands for protection. Great Britain took over Walvis Bay in 1878, and in 1884 Germany declared a protectorate over the region between the Orange and the Cunene (koo-NAE-nuh) Rivers. The Nama and Herero peoples resisted German rule for ten years.

Settlers from Germany began to arrive in what they called South-West Africa. Many established farms on Nama and Herero land. The Nama and Herero survived by working on their former lands for the German colonists. In 1903 the Germans announced that the Nama and Herero peoples should live in reserves, special areas that formed a very small part of the land these Africans had once owned.

In 1904 the Herero and the Nama rose in rebellions. The Germans forced the Herero into the Waterberg Mountains, killing thousands. Many Herero fled into the Kalahari (ka-luh-HAHR-ee) Desert, where they were left to die of thirst and hunger. About a thousand escaped to British-ruled Bechuanaland (see BOTSWANA). In 1905

Time line:	San hunter-gatherers living in southern Africa	Nama people move into area	Bantu-speaking people move into area	Frequent wars between Nama and Herero	South-West Africa becomes German protectorate
	ca. 18000 B.C.E.	ca. 300 B.C.E.	1400s C.E.	1800s	1884

only sixteen thousand Herero remained out of the previous population of eighty thousand. Nama resistance continued until 1907. Thousands of Nama died, many in concentration camps.

In 1915, during World War I, South African forces invaded South-West Africa and defeated the Germans. After the war ended, the League of Nations (an organization like the United Nations today) gave control of South-West Africa to neighboring British-ruled South Africa.

Many Germans remained in South-West Africa. The South African government encouraged thousands of Afrikaner (white, Afrikaans-speaking) farmers to move in to establish sheep and cattle ranches. The Africans were made to live in remote reserves where the land was poor. Mining companies exploited the copper mines in the north and the diamond mines on the coast. In the 1920s, groups of Nama and Rehobother (reh-BOE-ther), whose

ancestors were a mix of Afrikaner and Khoi-Khoi living around the town of Rehoboth, attempted to resist South African rule; both were harshly suppressed and many people were killed. In the 1930s a series of rebellions by the Ovambo people provided the main resistance to South Africa.

After World War II (1939–1945), the United Nations asked South Africa to prepare South-West Africa for independence. The South African government refused and treated South-West Africa as a part of its own country. It imposed racist policies, with harsh laws controlling where and how the Africans should live and work (see SOUTH AFRICA).

In 1960 the South-West African Peoples Organization (SWAPO) was launched and began guerrilla warfare against South African forces. South African rule came to an end only because of South African involvement in a civil war in Angola. In exchange for being allowed to rescue South African troops trapped in Angola while attacking SWAPO and African National Congress (ANC) guerrillas and refugee camps there, the South African government agreed to end its rule of Namibia. The country became independent in 1990 under President Sam Nujoma and the SWAPO party. Sam Nujoma and SWAPO were reelected by large majorities in 1994 and 1999.

Namibia's struggle for independence from South Africa was long and hard. This painted wall in the capital, Windhoek, celebrates that independence, achieved in 1990.

Nama and Herero people rebel; Herero rebellion crushed; over sixty thousand die	League of Nations hands over control of South-West Africa to South Africa	South-West African Peoples Organization (SWAPO) launched	Independence; SWAPO's Sam Nujoma becomes president
1904–1907	**1919**	**1960**	**1990**

The Peoples of Namibia

At least twenty-eight different languages are spoken in Namibia. As well as their own language, most people speak Afrikaans, the language of their former South African rulers, and many speak several local languages as well. The languages can be divided into two groups or families: Khoisan and Bantu. The Khoisan-speakers are the San, Nama, and Damara. No longer nomadic hunters and gatherers, the San work mainly as laborers on commercial farms; they are the poorest of Namibia's peoples. The Nama live mostly in the south, keeping cattle or working on white-owned farms. The Germans gave the Damara a homeland near the coast, but only a few live there today. Most have found work in the mines, on farms, or as laborers in the towns.

The biggest group of Bantu-speaking peoples is the Ovambo, making up half of the country's population. Eight different groups of Ovambo live in Namibia, each speaking a different dialect of their language, Oshivambo. Ovambo refugees from the civil war in Angola (see ANGOLA) fled to Namibia.

These subsistence farmers live in Ovamboland, an area of mixed wooded and dry grassland near the northern border between the Cunene and Okavango (oe-kah-VAHNG-goe) Rivers. In Ovamboland

Among the San people are individuals who are thought to have spiritual powers of healing. Here, the man, in a state of trance, is trying to heal the sick woman.

The San Way of Life

The San have lived in the driest areas of southern Africa for thousands of years.
Until recently they lived as nomadic hunter-gatherers, with an intimate knowledge of their environment. Each year they followed the same cycle, moving to places where the women knew they could find wild foods (melons, seeds, and nuts) and water for their families. Water was stored in ostrich shells. During the driest months they lived in small family groups, forming larger groups in the wet season, when food and water were more available. The men used bows and arrows to hunt larger wild animals, such as antelope, and trapped smaller game, such as tortoise. The whole band shared meat from the hunt. The San had plenty of time for leisure and made intricate beadwork aprons and headdresses.

each extended family or clan has its own compound, a small village surrounded by a fence and containing round or square thatched-roof houses. Farmlands encircle the villages. Women tend the crops of millet and corn, while men herd the cattle and goats. Many Ovambo men work farther south in industries, mines, and farms.

The second largest group are the Kavango (kah-VAHNG-goe). Groups of Kavango people also live in Botswana and Angola. Refugees from Angola, escaping the civil war, have also joined the Namibian Kavango. Living around the Okavango River, the Kavango are excellent fishers. They also grow crops and raise cattle.

In precolonial times the Herero people preferred keeping cattle to growing crops, but the Germans seized their lands and herds, and they were forced to become cattle hands on European farms or servants in the towns. Today most Herero live in towns.

A very small subgroup of the Herero called the Himba (HEEM-bah), or Ovahimba, live in the Kaokoveld, raising cattle. The women wear short leather skirts and jewelry made from iron and shells and smear their skin with butter, ash, and ocher, an earthy iron ore.

The people of mixed race speak Afrikaans and/or English. The white people mostly speak Afrikaans or German, own most of the commercial farms, and live on the central plateau, mostly around Windhoek (vint-HUHK).

Namibia Today

Most Namibians are Christian. Of these, around half (mainly the Ovambo) are Lutheran, and about one-fifth are Roman Catholic. Of the rest, some belong to the

Herero women still wear their own colorful version of the clothes that German missionaries introduced in the 1800s, with many layers of petticoats and horn-shaped headdresses.

Dutch Reformed Church (which originated in South Africa), some are Calvinist, and some are Anglican. The influence of older African religions remains strong in some areas. For example, the Ovambo keep a sacred fire burning in the middle of their villages, and the Himba have sacred places that are used for religious ceremonies.

After independence, money was poured into education. Now more than 85 percent of children attend school. The emphasis in current health policies is on using mobile clinics to provide preventive health care. Two-thirds of the people are very poor, and malnutrition is common. Namibia has one of the highest rates of HIV infection and AIDS in Africa. Average life expectancy for men is forty-two years, for women forty-one.

Namibia is rich in minerals, and the country's exports include diamonds from the south, as well as uranium, tin, tungsten, and copper. Gold and natural gas are also becoming important mineral products.

The most important industry is fishing and fish processing. Lobsters, sardines, and pilchards caught in the Atlantic Ocean are processed mostly at Walvis Bay and Lüderitz (LOO-duh-rits).

So much of Namibia is desert that little land is suitable for growing crops. The commercial ranches north and south of Windhoek produce beef and mutton. In the north people live mostly by subsistence farming, growing millet, sorghum, corn, and peanuts.

One-third of Namibia's population lives in Windhoek and other towns. The

buildings and culture of Windhoek, Swakopmund (SFAH-kawp-muhnt), and Lüderitz show a strong German influence. The Africans who live in the towns have largely adopted Western dress and ways.

The food people eat varies depending on their way of life. The staple food of the Ovambo is cornmeal porridge called *mielie pap* (MEE-lee pap). They also eat millet made into soup or porridge, eaten with fish or meat stew. People who live in the dry areas have learned to find other food sources; for example, the Nama eat the flesh of spiny, round melons. The cattle-keeping Herero eat meat and dairy products.

All the peoples make goods from leather, including blankets and items of

clothing. Many northern groups, such as the Ovambo and Kavango, fashion baskets from strips of palm leaves. Wood carving is also common among the northern peoples. They make a wide range of items, including musical instruments and toys, often highly decorated.

Music and dance are part of daily life. When the community gathers, maybe for a wedding, everyone joins in the dancing. The instruments used are drums, bows, rattles, harps, marimbas, and thumb pianos made from wood or a gourd and tuned metal or wooden strips that are plucked. The Nama have a strong tradition of religious singing in four-part harmony, and choral music is very popular among the white population.

This area of Windhoek is home for people who have recently come to the city. Some houses are shanties, but each family receives its own plot and has access to piped water.

NIGER

NIGER IS A LARGE, LANDLOCKED NATION IN NORTHWESTERN AFRICA.

In the north of Niger stand high plateaus and sand dunes, part of the Sahara Desert. In the center a range of mountains known as the Aïr Massif rises to 3,520 feet (1,073 meters). In the south, in the Sahel, are high, dry plateau lands. Some well-watered, fertile soil lies beside the Niger River and Lake Chad.

CLIMATE

Niger has a hot, dry climate. In the south a short rainy season lasts from June to October. The northern desert region receives almost no rain.

Average January temperature: 59°F (15°C)
Average July temperature: 93°F (34°C)
Average annual precipitation: 22 in. (56 cm)

As choking desert dust swirls in the air, a Wodaabe herdsman rounds up his cattle and moves them to fresh pastures on the edge of the Sahara Desert.

Northern Nomads and Southern Farmers

Thousands of years ago, hunters and cattle herders lived among the trees and grasses of the Sahara. Then the climate changed, the Sahara region grew drier, and by around 3000 B.C.E. a vast area of desert separated present-day Niger (NIE-juhr) from the north.

From around 300 C.E. merchants from northern Africa began to make regular trading expeditions across the Sahara. Salt from Niger was a valuable commodity, traded for gold and slaves with peoples farther south.

By around 700, Berber states based in Morocco (see MOROCCO) ruled western

FACTS AND FIGURES

Official name: *République du Niger*

Status: *Independent state*

Capital: *Niamey*

Major towns: *Zinder, Agadez*

Area: *459,073 square miles (1,188,999 square kilometers)*

Population: *10,000,000*

Population density: *22 per square mile (8 per square kilometer)*

Peoples: *56 percent Hausa; 22 percent Djerma-Songhai; 9 percent Fulani; 4 percent Kanuri-Beriberi; 9 percent Tuareg and others*

Official language: *French*

Currency: *CFA franc*

National days: *Independence Day (August 3); Republic Day (December 18)*

Country's name: *The country takes its name from the Niger River. Niger means "black" in Latin, the language of the Romans, but it is not known why the river got this name.*

Niger. Gradually the Berbers introduced their Muslim faith to most of Niger.

Around 1000 the rich Kanem-Bornu Empire, which ruled the eastern Sahel region (see CHAD and NIGERIA), took over eastern Niger. Hausa (HOW-sah) farmers from northern Nigeria also arrived to settle in southwestern Niger, attracted by fertile land beside the Niger River. From around 1500, southern Niger was divided among Hausa city-states, which grew rich through trade. The Hausa were followed, around 1600, by groups of Songhai (SAWNG-hae) and Djerma (JER-mah) people, who fled from Mali after the Songhai Empire (see MALI) collapsed. Between 1804 and 1810 Fulani (foo-LAH-nee) armies from Nigeria, led by a Muslim religious teacher, Usman dan Fodio, conquered Hausa lands in southern Niger (see NIGERIA).

To the north of the Hausa lived the Tuareg (TWAHR-ehg), desert people of Berber origin who controlled the trans-Saharan trade routes. They established their own state, the Sultanate of Aïr, around present-day Agadez in the 1400s. During the 1700s and 1800s, Aïr expanded and became an important state in the region.

In about 1854 France organized army expeditions to conquer Niger. During the 1890s the French signed treaties with the Hausa, Songhai, and Fulani leaders and built a fort at Niamey (NYAH-mae). The Tuareg people refused to accept French rule and fought the French fiercely for more than twenty years. Nonetheless, in 1922 Niger became a French colony.

Compared with France's other African colonies farther to the west, Niger did not attract many European settlers. During the 1930s French colonists set up peanut farming projects with little success. French rulers did almost nothing to help the people of Niger; health care and education were minimal, and most families remained very poor. After the end of World War II (1939–1945), politicians in Niger began to demand independence.

In 1960 France allowed Niger to become independent, along with other French colonies in western Africa. In 1968 uranium was discovered in Niger, and the future looked bright. However, that same

Time line:	Hunters and cattle herders live in Sahara region	Berbers rule western Niger	Eastern Niger becomes part of Kanem-Bornu Empire	Tuareg Sultanate of Aïr established	Songhai and Djerma peoples arrive from Mali
	ca. 5000 B.C.E.	ca. 700 C.E.	ca. 1000	1400s	ca. 1600

This Tuareg man, riding a well-dressed camel, has traveled across the desert to watch camel races near I-n-Gall, in central Niger, the Tuareg's homeland for hundreds of years.

uranium boom was short-lived; prices collapsed in 1979, leaving the government almost bankrupt.

From 1983 to 1985 further terrible droughts plagued the land, and the Niger River stopped flowing. The government's strict economic policies, aimed at reducing its debts, led to riots and violent protests. In 1990 the Tuareg demanded an independent homeland and rebelled.

In 1992 a democratic, multiparty constitution was introduced, but the economy was in a state of crisis, with massive government debts. Workers and students continued to protest, and the Tuareg rebels were still strong. Gangs of armed bandits attacked anyone venturing into the northern region. The Tuareg rebellion ended in 1995 when the Tuareg signed a peace accord with the government.

In 1996 there was a military coup. Alarmed by this political turmoil, overseas donors stopped sending aid. In April 1999 another coup occurred, and the president was assassinated. A new president, Mamadou Tandja, was elected in November 1999. In the light of recent history, however, the future remains uncertain.

Niger's Peoples

Ninety percent of Niger's people live in the southern and central regions. The north is too dry for anyone, except a few nomads, to survive. As a general rule, each people is based in a distinct region, but in recent years, members of many different ethnic groups have moved to towns, hoping to find work.

year, the first of many severe droughts hit the Sahel region on the Sahara's fringes. Almost two-thirds of Niger's cattle, sheep, and goats died, and many people faced starvation. International agencies provided food and shelter for refugees.

The drought ended in 1974. At the same time world prices for uranium rose fivefold, making the government very rich, but money from uranium did not help ordinary people. Many became worse off, as prices of food and fuel rose by 25 percent. The

Fulani armies conquer Hausa states	Tuareg fight French in north	Niger becomes French colony	Niger becomes independent	Severe droughts	Rebellions by Tuareg groups in north	Economic crisis and political instability
1804–1810	1898–1920	1922	1960	1960s–1980s	1990–1995	1996–1999

The Hausa people make up over half the population. Today they continue their long established occupations as traders in busy commercial centers such as Maradi (mah-RAH-dee) and Zinder (ZIN-duhr) and as farmers. The Hausa also live across the border in neighboring Nigeria (see NIGERIA). Around the shores of Lake Chad in eastern Niger, Hausa men and women have married members of the indigenous Kanuri (kah-NOO-ree) people, one of the smallest groups within Niger. People of mixed Kanuri and Hausa ancestry are often known as Beriberi (beh-ree-BEH-ree). In the past, the Kanuri and Beriberi lived by farming and fishing. Today many have moved to towns.

The next largest groups are the Djerma and the Songhai, who are closely related and speak similar languages. The Djerma live in and around the capital city, Niamey. The Songhai live mostly along the Niger River. The Djerma-Songhai have been the most powerful group in Niger's government for almost one hundred years. Today they hold many of the top government jobs. Unlike other black African peoples in the country, they were offered the chance of education by French colonial rulers. This was because they lived around Niamey, the French center of administration, one of the few places the French built schools for the local people.

For centuries Fulani people have followed a variety of lifestyles. Some are farmers and traders who live in villages and towns in the central region. Others, known in Niger as the Wodaabe (woe-DAH-bee), live as nomadic cattle herders

A family relaxes in a comfortably furnished home in the Hausa trading city of Zinder. The curved roof is designed for coolness; temperatures here can reach over 100°F (38°C).

on the dry grasslands bordering the desert west of Agadez.

The Tuareg also follow a nomadic lifestyle, moving between oases in search of water for their camels or feeding their animals on the dry, dusty grassland along the desert's edge (see ALGERIA). Since the recent droughts, which destroyed vast areas of grazing, some Tuareg families have been forced to move to refugee camps and tent cities on the edges of towns.

Niger Today

Although French is the official language of Niger, it is spoken mostly by educated people and government officials. Ordinary people speak their own local language or Hausa, which is used as a common tongue by merchants and market traders.

About four out of every five people in Niger are Muslim; the rest of the population follow African religions that include belief in a creator god and in spirits in the natural world. In recent years groups of Muslim

These painted village homes are made of mud on a wooden frame. Newer homes are built from concrete and roofed with sheet metal.

including teachers, civil servants, and the police, total about 4 percent of the workforce.

Typical meals in Niger are based on boiled starchy foods—millet, rice, cornmeal, and beans called *niebé* (NYEH-bae), which are eaten with a vegetable sauce. Families add meat if they can afford it or fish if they live close to a river or lake. Small pieces of beef and mutton are grilled over open fires as kebabs and eaten as street food in Hausa regions. Food eaten by the Tuareg includes dates, yogurt, rice, and mutton.

For dessert, people eat tropical fruits grown in the south, such as bananas, papayas, mangoes, and guavas. In addition they also eat fresh and dried dates from northern oases or sweet sticky dumplings called *foura* (FOO-rah), made from millet mixed with sugar, milk, and spices. The most popular drink is hot, sweet tea, served without milk.

fundamentalists have criticized the government for ignoring spiritual values.

About half of all adults survive by growing food and raising animals for themselves and their families to eat. Ninety percent of employed people also work on the land. Farmers in the north raise livestock. In the south they grow millet, rice, sorghum, tropical fruits, and vegetables, plus peanuts, cotton, and cowpeas (also known as black-eyed peas) for export. During the 1970s the government spent money on improving agriculture, especially on irrigation projects. As a result, farmers can grow crops to feed the whole population, except in major drought years.

About 6 percent of workers have jobs in industry or as traders. Factories produce goods for local use, such as peanut oil, cotton cloth, and cement. Today mining employs few people, even though Niger has some of the richest uranium deposits in the world. Government employees,

Housing styles and building materials vary according to local conditions. In the desert and dry Sahel grasslands, nomads live in tents made of goatskin or woven camel hair. In wetter grassland regions and in farming villages farther south, older homes are made of sun-dried mud bricks or mud and chopped straw on a wooden frame. Usually they are built as a series of single rooms around a central courtyard.

In towns like Agadez, fine old examples of large Hausa buildings, including many mosques, still stand. They have plastered mud brick walls, with spiny permanent scaffolding sticking out at right angles, and carved wooden windows and doors. In the town of Zinder, elaborate painted patterns decorate some houses.

The peoples of Niger produce arts and crafts in a variety of styles. The Tuareg are skilled at silversmithing and leather work. Cross-shaped pendants are especially famous, as are Tuareg swords. Fulani artisans weave patterned blankets in subtle colors from sheep's wool. The Hausa are admired for fine leather goods and for decorated calabashes (water containers made from dried gourds). Brightly colored Djerma cloths made from strips of cotton fabric sewn together are highly prized.

Poverty, poor diet, and a harsh environment make Niger an unhealthy place to live. Few doctors and hospitals exist outside towns. On average, a man or woman today can expect to live only forty-two years. One in every eight babies does not survive to reach its first birthday.

Although schooling is free and compulsory for children ages six to fifteen, less than one-third of all children attend school. Some live too far away from the nearest school, some are too poor to pay for equipment, others are needed to work in their family's fields. Because of this, only about 21 percent of men and 7 percent of women can read and write. This difference exists because traditionally it was not considered worthwhile or respectable to send girls to school.

Gerewol: The Bridegroom Parade

Gerewol (GEHR-wawl) is a week-long festival, that originated when groups of nomadic Wodaabe (Fulani) cattle-herding families brought their animals to lick salty grass on the edge of the desert. Salt is essential for the animals' health.

Today Gerewol is famous for the social rituals that take place at the same time. Young, unmarried Wodaabe men dress themselves up in their best clothes and jewelry, paint their faces, and carefully arrange their hair. They parade and dance in front of all the young women, hoping to be chosen as husbands. Some men let themselves be beaten with sticks to show how tough and brave they are. If a young woman likes the look of a young man, she picks him out of the parade and takes him to her parents. They then agree on a bride price to be given to the bride's parents, and a marriage is arranged.

Young Wodaabe men, adorned with beads and turbans, dance at the annual Gerewol festival to attract young, unmarried women.

NIGERIA

THE FEDERAL REPUBLIC OF NIGERIA HAS THE GREATEST POPULATION OF ANY COUNTRY IN AFRICA.

Much of the south of Nigeria is dense rain forest. Moving north, the forest begins to give way to savanna. The land here is typical of much of tropical Africa, with scattered trees, bushes, and grassland. The far north has become much drier in recent years, and droughts have been severe. In the far northeast the savanna gradually slopes down into marshes surrounding Lake Chad, a freshwater lake that Nigeria shares with Cameroon, Chad, and Niger.

The Niger River, one of the great rivers of Africa, enters Nigeria from Niger and flows to the Atlantic Ocean. Before it reaches the sea, it divides into many small rivers and channels that form the Niger Delta. A major tributary of the Niger is the Benue River, which flows from the east for over 600 miles (960 kilometers) to join the Niger.

CLIMATE

Nigeria is humid in the south, becoming increasingly dry to the north. During December and January a dry wind known as the harmattan blows in from the Sahara Desert, bringing cool nights and a fine covering of sand and dust across the land.

	Lagos	Kano
Average January temperature:	81°F (27°C)	70°F (21°C)
Average July temperature:	78°F (26°C)	79°F (26°C)
Average annual precipitation:	72 in. (183 cm)	35 in. (89 cm)

Early Societies

The first people who lived in what is now Nigeria (nie-JIR-ee-uh) were hunter-gatherers. They made tools and weapons of stone and lived by hunting animals, gathering wild fruits and vegetables, and catching fish in local rivers. Toward the end of the Stone Age (about 5000 B.C.E.), some peoples began to practice agriculture and settle in villages. In the savanna region people kept cattle and grew millet and rice, which were originally wild grasses. On the forest edges they cultivated yams (a root vegetable) and palm nuts (from palm trees).

About twenty-five hundred years ago, the knowledge of ironworking spread in the region. Iron tools made clearing vegetation and digging wells for water much easier. People could grow more food and their populations expanded. Not everyone was needed to farm. Some people could become specialists, such as artisans, traders, priests, and rulers.

Knowledge of this early history of Nigeria is sketchy. Evidence of Stone Age and Iron Age people has been found, mostly in the form of stone ax heads and iron-smelting furnaces. The most important find to date is at the village of Nok in central Nigeria. Here, iron-smelting furnaces and fine terra-cotta sculptures have been found. The Nok culture flourished between about 400 B.C.E. and 200 C.E.

FACTS AND FIGURES

Official name: Federal Republic of Nigeria

Status: Independent state

Capital: Abuja

Major towns: Lagos, Ibadan, Ogbomosho, Kano, Ilorin, Port Harcourt, Zaria

Area: 356,669 square miles (923,773 square kilometers)

Population: 113,800,000

Population density: 319 per square mile (123 per square kilometer)

Peoples: Estimated to be more than 250 different ethnic groups. The four largest groups, the Hausa, Fulani, Yoruba, and Igbo, make up about 70 percent of the population.

Official language: English

Currency: Naira

National day: Independence Day (October 1)

Country's name: Nigeria takes its name from the Niger River. Niger means "black" in Latin, the language of the Romans, but it is not known why the river got this name.

Little else is known about the history of Nigeria during the first thousand years C.E. Bronze objects found at Igbo-Ukwo (EE-boe-ook-woe) in the forests of the south are believed to be

A life-size terra-cotta head found during excavations at Nok. The quality of the sculpture shows that the Nok people were skilled artisans.

Time line:	Hunter-gathers live in the region	People begin to grow crops and keep cattle	Ironworking spreads across region
	before 5000 B.C.E.	**ca. 5000 B.C.E.**	**ca. 500 B.C.E.**

383

The emir, or ruler, of Katsina rides in a procession during the Muslim festival of Sallah. Katsina was one of the most powerful Hausa states between 1500 and 1800.

burial objects of a leader who lived in the late ninth century. The copper used to make them must have come from Saharan mines in present-day Niger, so forest peoples must have had contact with the long-distance trading networks to the north.

Savanna States of the North

The lands of Nigeria were not part of the great empires of the savanna—Ghana, Mali, and Songhai—that flourished between the seventh and sixteenth centuries (see MALI). However, the influence of these empires was felt in the north through trans-Saharan trade and the gradual spread of Islam. Arab traders from northern Africa bought gold from western Africa in exchange for cloth, copper beads, weapons, and salt. The influence of these Muslim traders also encouraged people to convert to Islam.

The savanna states of northern Nigeria were Kanem-Bornu and the Hausa states. Kanem-Bornu (KAH-nehm-BOER-noo) began as Kanem, northeast of Lake Chad, outside what is modern Nigeria, in the ninth or tenth century. During the fourteenth century the nomadic people of

Nok culture: settled community using iron	Origin of Kanem state	Igbo-Ukwo culture flourishes	Trans-Saharan trade grows, bringing Islam to northern peoples; origins of first Hausa and Yoruba states
ca. 400 B.C.E.–200 C.E.	ca. 800 C.E.	ca. 900	ca. 1000–1100

Amina: Queen of the Hausa

During the sixteenth century the Hausa state of Zaria was ruled by a woman, Queen Amina. For thirty-four years she led her armies into battle against her enemies and won victory after victory. To protect the people of Zaria from enemy attack, Amina had huge walls built all around the town. These walls still stand today, and the people of Zaria call the walls after Queen Amina.

Kanem moved to Bornu, southwest of Lake Chad, to take advantage of its more fertile grasslands and better access to the Hausa trade routes. The Kanuri (kah-NOO-ree) people of today are descended from marriages between the peoples from Kanem and Bornu. Kanem-Bornu reached its height in the sixteenth century.

The first Hausa (HOW-sah) settlements were established during the eleventh and twelfth centuries. Fertile farmland and trade across the Sahara Desert allowed small Hausa towns to grow larger and wealthier. As the towns grew, their citizens built protective walls around them and began to rule the people living in the surrounding area. Such towns grew into small states during the 1300s. Between 1500 and 1800 the most powerful of these states were Kano (KAH-noe), Katsina (KAHT-see-nah), and Zaria (ZAHR-ee-uh). Their rulers became converts to Islam, and, gradually, so did their peoples.

Forest States of the South

The most important of the early forest states of western Africa were found in what today is the southern part of Nigeria. From about the eleventh century, the Yoruba (YOE-roo-bah) people began to organize themselves in towns. These towns gradually grew into small states, such as Ife (EE-fae), which lay in an area of fertile soil and high rainfall, suitable for growing crops and raising domestic animals. Many artifacts of wood, ivory, bronze, copper, brass, and terra-cotta, dating from the twelfth to fifteenth centuries, have been found at Ife. The Yoruba founded the state of Oyo (OY-oe) in the 1300s, and by the fifteenth century Oyo had become more powerful than Ife. The location of Oyo to

The Ife Creation Legend

The Yoruba people tell how the first human beings came to Ife. In the beginning the world was a "watery waste." God ordered his son Oduduwa to climb down from the heavens on a chain and to carry with him a handful of earth, a rooster, and a palm nut. At the foot of the chain, Oduduwa scattered the earth on the water and created the first land at Ife. The rooster then scratched a hole in the earth and into the hole Oduduwa planted the palm nut. From this grew an enormous tree with sixteen branches, and from each branch came a king of the Yoruba states.

Rise of Ife and Benin; Kanem-Bornu expands	Yoruba state of Oyo founded	Benin at its height	Portuguese arrive in Benin	Increasing trade contacts with Europeans
ca. 1100–1300	1300s	ca. 1400–1500	1485	1600–1800

the north of Ife, on the fringes of the forest and savanna, meant that it was able to control the southern end of the trans-Saharan trade. The army kept horses and built up a powerful cavalry. For nearly four hundred years, Oyo expanded and became the most powerful of the forest states. Oyo developed a unique system of government in which checks on the power of the king meant that no one person in the state could become too powerful.

By the mid-fifteenth century, the Edo (EE-doe) people of the state of Benin (bae-NEEN), to the southeast of Ife, had

A bronze plaque that decorated the palace walls of Benin's kings. It celebrates their power and authority; here, the king, dressed for battle, towers over his tiny subjects.

conquered many lands and had become rich and powerful through the trans-Saharan trade. In the late fifteenth century, when Benin was at its height, its wealth was shown in the splendor of the city of Benin, with its wide streets, its houses with finely carved doors, and the beautiful art in brass, bronze, and ivory that its artisans produced.

Communities without Kings

The dense forests behind the mangrove swamps and tidal creeks of the Niger Delta were home to the Igbo (EE-boe) people. They lived in village societies. Each of the thousands of densely populated villages ruled itself. They had no kings or rulers. Instead every man, but not one woman, had the right to voice his opinion on public affairs at the village assembly. When particularly important decisions had to be made, the ancestors were called upon. Leading clan members dressed as *egwugwu* (ehg-WOOG-woo), or ancestral spirits. Their decisions could not be questioned.

Each Igbo village had links with other villages. They traded peacefully with each other and believed in the same gods. Each village or group of villages had skilled artisans in weaving, woodworking, and metalworking.

The Tiv (TIV) people of east-central Nigeria did not have states or rulers either. They lived in family compounds, near people closely related to them. In each of these compounds, authority came from the head of the family, who was always a man. He organized farmwork and settled any disputes within the family.

Oyo power grows	Usman dan Fodio leads Fulani in holy war against Hausa states, establishes united Fulani Empire	Oyo collapses; civil war in Yorubaland	Niger Delta city-states grow
1700s	**1804–1808**	**1813–1837**	**1830s–1840s**

Change and Conquest

The Portuguese were the first Europeans to sail around the coast of western Africa in the fifteenth century. They began to trade with the coastal people, selling cheap iron, cloth, copper, and guns in exchange for ivory, gold, and pepper. They—and other Europeans, such as the Dutch, British, and French—soon began to buy human beings as well. They wanted slaves to work on their new sugar and tobacco plantations in North America and the Caribbean. Many African traders were happy to sell slaves to Europeans because they knew it would make them rich and powerful. Most slaves were caught in village raids or during wars.

The slave trade was finally abolished in the nineteenth century. By then many millions of western African people had died, been sold into slavery, or had lost their families and communities.

Islam had been part of the way of life in the north for several centuries. Many people, especially the rulers of the Hausa states, called themselves Muslim, but they mixed Islam with traditional religions and did not follow Islamic holy law in their daily lives. Truly religious Muslims, found mostly among the Fulani (foo-LAH-nee) and Kanuri people, were horrified at the way Islam was being corrupted. It was from the Fulani that Usman dan Fodio came, a man of great learning and the leader of the jihad, or holy war, against the rulers of the Hausa states.

Early in the nineteenth century, Usman dan Fodio and his followers conquered the weak, divided Hausa states and established a united Fulani Empire, which covered most of northern Nigeria. The empire stayed united and powerful throughout the nineteenth century. It also encouraged more people to convert to Islam and helped spread Islamic education.

European influence hardly touched the north, but it was different in the south. By

Olaudah Equiano

Slaves were rarely able to speak out about their lives. But in 1789 Olaudah Equiano published the story of his life. As a young boy, he had lived happily with his family in Igboland, a land "uncommonly rich and fruitful." When he was eleven, African slave dealers kidnapped him and his sister. They were taken to the coast and put on a slave ship. As the ship crossed the Atlantic, ". . . the air became unfit to breathe and many of the slaves fell sick and died. Our wretched situation was aggravated by the heavy chains on our legs, the filth of the necessary tubs, and the shrieks of the women and the groans of the dying."

In North America Olaudah was sold to a plantation owner. He found the life of a plantation slave hard and cruel. Later he was sold to a new master in England, where, at the age of twenty-one, he was able to buy his freedom. He married an English woman, became active in the movement to abolish slavery, and wrote his life story.

Nigeria brought under British control	Nigeria becomes a British colony	Beginning and growth of Nigerian nationalism	Political parties formed, begin campaign for independent Nigeria
1861–1910	1914	1920s	1940–1960

the nineteenth century European slave traders had been replaced by other traders and by missionaries, mostly from Great Britain.

The once-powerful states of Benin and Oyo were in decline. Between 1813 and 1837, Oyo collapsed, and civil war spread throughout Yoruba lands. In the Niger Delta, city-states, especially Bonny and Brass, based their power first on the slave trade and then on trading in palm oil, which was used as a lubricant for industrial machinery in factories throughout Europe.

The British wanted to be sure that trade was peaceful and beneficial for them. In the second half of the nineteenth century they began to take control in different parts of Nigeria, including the lands of the Fulani and Yoruba, and the Niger Delta.

By the early twentieth century, all of Nigeria—some areas taken by force and some by peaceful means—was under the control of the British.

The Years of British Rule

From 1914 the British controlled the country through a system known as Indirect Rule. They believed that the best and cheapest way to govern Africans was through their own rulers, with the British

A carved panel from the palace door of the Yoruba ruler of Ikere Ekiti. It shows the arrival in 1895 of the first British district commissioner, carried by African servants.

at the top. Indirect Rule suited the rulers of the Hausa states because it often increased their power.

However, Indirect Rule did not work as well in southern Nigeria. Among the Igbo, the British made certain men "warrant chiefs" (by virtue of a warrant, or written authority) and gave them power over people who had always seen themselves as equal.

From the 1920s Nigerians began to campaign for an end to colonial rule. World War II (1939–1945) was a turning point. Nigeria supplied raw materials and

Nigeria becomes an independent nation	Military coups and ethnic conflict	Civil war as Igbo fight for Biafran independence; Biafrans defeated	Years of oil wealth and military coups
1960	**1966**	**1967–1970**	**1970–1979**

soldiers for the British war effort. After the war, these soldiers wanted a better deal.

Political parties formed, most based on the main ethnic groups, and they campaigned for an independent Nigeria. Power was handed over in stages, with full independence in 1960.

Independence and Beyond

Northerners dominated the government of newly independent Nigeria. This created suspicion and fear in the other regions. In 1966 there were two bloody military coups and ever-growing conflict between the major ethnic groups. The Hausa and other northerners feared that the Igbo in the south were taking control. Igbo living in the north were attacked and many were killed. Thousands fled south, terrified for their lives.

In 1967 the Igbo declared their own independent state of Biafra (bee-AH-fruh). Their leader, Colonel Emeka Ojukwu, believed that the rest of Nigeria was too divided to fight against Biafra and that the recently discovered oil in the Niger Delta would provide the wealth to run their economy.

However, Ojukwu was wrong. The government wished to seize Igbo lands in the Niger Delta to deprive the Igbo of oil revenues. The conflict resulted in a long, hard-fought war between the Igbo and the rest of Nigeria. More than half a million people died. The Igbo fought bravely but were finally defeated in 1970. They feared terrible revenge, but not one Biafran was executed for treason. Though many

problems remained, Nigeria was now a united country.

Civilian rule returned for just four years, from 1979 to 1983, when the military took power again. During the 1980s and much of the 1990s, in spite of promises to hand over power to democratic government, the military remained in charge.

In 1993 General Sani Abacha seized power. Under his rule all opposition was brutally suppressed, and the Nigerian economy continued to decline. Abacha died in 1997, and his successor agreed that elections should be held in 1998 and 1999.

In May 1999 a former military leader, Olesegun Obasanjo (who had been jailed under Abacha's regime), was sworn in as the democratically elected president. He immediately began to clean up the corruption of the previous years (much of Nigeria's oil earnings had poured into the hands of government officials).

Early hopes of a period of peaceful reconstruction were thrown into doubt at the end of 1999, however, when one of the northern states of the Nigerian federation, Zamfara, introduced a legal system based upon Islamic holy laws in an attempt to combat rising rates of crime. This prompted other northern states to talk of following their example, to the consternation of the large Christian minorities in many of these states. Distrust and demonstrations soon turned to violence, leaving many Christians and Muslims dead in both northern and southern states. Clearly the new government faced a great challenge in restoring peace and avoiding the breakup of this vast federation of peoples.

Civilian rule	Years of military rule; Nigerian oil wealth declines	General Sani Abacha in power; all opposition suppressed	Return to democracy; Olesegun Obasanjo elected president
1979–1983	**1980s–1990s**	**1993–1997**	**1999**

Igbo women from eastern Nigeria. This popular style of dress, with brightly colored head ties, blouses, and wraparound skirts, is practical and cool.

Peoples and Languages

Nigeria is a great mixture of peoples, languages, and cultures. There are estimated to be at least 250 different ethnic groups. About two-thirds of all Nigerians are from four main groups: the Hausa and Fulani in the north, the Yoruba in the west, and the Igbo in the east.

Though English is the official language, there are as many languages as there are ethnic groups. Most Nigerians speak at least three: their own local language, the main language of the wider area they live in, and English. Hausa is probably spoken by more people than any other Nigerian language. People from the south may also speak Pidgin, which mixes English with local languages. Pidgin is often used for trade when the people trading cannot understand each other's language.

Many Religions in One Nation

The main religions in Nigeria are Islam, which is practiced mostly in the north, and Christianity, practiced mostly in the south. It is estimated that approximately 47 percent of Nigerians are Muslim and 35 percent are Christian. Just under one-fifth of the population follows traditional African religions.

Nigerian Muslims are mostly found among the Hausa and Fulani peoples. They follow the same practices as their millions of Muslim brothers and sisters throughout the world. The Muslim tradition of learning, including studying theology, the law, mathematics, and science, is also important to them. Mosques are the center of a Muslim's life; they range from simple mud buildings in villages and towns to the beautiful architecture of modern mosques in cities such as Lagos (LAE-gahs).

Aladura Churches

In western Africa independent Christian churches mix African customs with the Christian faith. Many believers find these mixed beliefs more appropriate and more meaningful than Western-style Christianity. Aladura (ah-lah-DOO-rah), which means "praying people," churches were started by Yoruba Christians in Nigeria and have spread along the western African coast. The service in an aladura church is full of joy and praise for God. The congregation sings and dances, accompanied by drumming. Some worshipers become so moved that they pass into a trance. The leaders of such churches are often believed to have spiritual healing powers.

Some Muslim women still live in purdah, which means that they cannot leave their houses except at night and then they must be veiled. However, in many cases women are needed to work on the farm or they choose to be part of the wider community. Few such women wear veils.

Missionaries from Europe introduced Christianity to Nigeria. Most Igbo and Yoruba people today are Christian. Many belong to Roman Catholic or Protestant churches, but some have set up their own churches that are more African.

There are many different African religions in Nigeria, with many and varied beliefs and practices. They all share a core belief in an all-powerful creator god who cannot be worshiped directly but must be worshiped through many lesser gods.

The Yoruba call their all-powerful god Olorun (OE-loe-roon), which means "the owner of the sky." He made the earth and the first people on earth. Hundreds of lesser gods are known as *orisa* (oe-RIH-sah). These include Ogun (OE-goon), the god of war, who brought iron to the Yoruba. Believed to be the god of traditional war chiefs and of blacksmiths, Ogun has recently been adopted by taxi and truck drivers as their god too. Shango (SHANG-goe) is the god of thunder and lightning; several of his wives are river goddesses. Eshu (AE-shoo) is the messenger of the gods, a trickster god but also the guardian of houses and villages.

Part of a sacred shrine for Oshun, a Yoruba river goddess, at Oshogbo (oe-SHOEG-boe) in western Nigeria. The flowing lines of the building echo the movement of the river.

The Igbo call their all-powerful god Chukwu (CHOOK-woo). Chukwu gives everyone on earth *chi* (CHEE). Chi is responsible for all the good and bad things a person does in life. Of all the other Igbo gods, the most important is Ala (AH-lah),

391

Nigeria's rapidly increasing population means that many forests are cut and burned to provide land for growing crops. Unfortunately, the thin soil is soon exhausted.

the earth goddess and Chukwu's messenger. The center of most Igbo villages has a shrine to Ala.

Oracles are very important to the Igbo and are believed to have great powers. Igbo oracles are shrines where a person can appeal to a god for help in times of trouble. Offerings are made through the priest, who then gives the verdict of the god.

Economy and Resources

Nigeria is rich in natural resources—in its land and its forests, in its minerals, and in its rivers and lakes. It has the potential to be one of Africa's richest nations.

Workers on an oil rig in the Niger Delta. Oil has modernized Nigeria and brought great wealth to some, but it has also polluted the water for the people living in the delta.

Nearly half of all Nigerians live by farming. The main crops grown in the north are peanuts, cotton, sorghum, and millet. In the south the farmers grow cocoa, palm oil, rice, and the root vegetables cassava and yam. Forests provide rubber and timber.

Nigeria has experienced more industrial development than most African countries. Manufacturing industries include oil refineries, textiles, food processing, brewing, cement production, and motor-vehicle assembly.

Mineral resources include oil, natural gas, tin, columbite, and coal. Of these, oil is by far the most valuable. It was discovered in large quantities deep beneath the swamps of the Niger Delta in the 1960s. By the 1970s, Nigeria was one of the largest oil producers in the world and by far the richest country in western Africa.

Nigerians came to depend on oil money, and ambitious government plans for new

development were based entirely upon it. The government neglected agriculture, and many people left farming to seek their fortunes in the cities. As a result, Nigeria, which has rich farmland, has had to import basic foods such as rice and peanut oil.

During the 1980s a drop in the world price of oil and corruption in the oil industry led to a near collapse of the Nigerian economy. The government was forced to introduce tough economic measures to repay the country's debts. During the 1990s Nigeria worked to reduce its dependence on oil by extracting more natural gas and by refining different products from oil. People have been encouraged to grow more crops so that the country can become self-sufficient in food once again.

However, life is still hard for ordinary Nigerians. Many live in great poverty and cannot find work, especially in the fast-growing towns and cities.

The medical school at Benin University. Most of these students will end up as doctors in city hospitals. Few will be tempted to work in rural clinics with poor facilities.

Education and Health

The literacy rate in Nigeria is estimated to be just under 57 percent for men and 47 percent for women; the difference is due to the lack of importance families placed on education for their female children. Elementary education is free and compulsory, although in practice not all children go to school. Children attend elementary school for six years and are taught in their own language or the first language of the region in which they live. This system of universal primary education was introduced during the oil boom years of the 1970s.

Places in secondary school are more limited. Schools are often overcrowded, and trained teachers are in short supply. Secondary education lasts for six years,

Children with their teacher at a nursery school. Their education will probably follow a Western-style system, similar to that introduced by British missionaries during the 1800s.

school. Such schools are run by *mallams* (mah-LAHMZ), volunteer religious teachers, either in the local mosque, the mallam's house, or outdoors. Children learn the Arabic alphabet and to read the Koran, along with the meaning and spiritual values of Islam.

Informal education aims to teach children to be good and useful members of their community. Basic skills and knowledge are learned within the family: farming techniques, domestic tasks, making things to sell, and trading skills. Customs and morals of the culture are often passed on through games, riddles, and songs. Outside the family, children may be apprenticed to a skilled adult. This apprenticeship system includes modern skills, such as truck driving and building, plus specialized skills, such as leather working, cloth dyeing, and blacksmithing.

Life expectancy in Nigeria averages fifty-three years. Since independence, health care facilities have expanded greatly. There have been great efforts to provide primary health care in towns and villages. However, many problems must still be overcome. The economic problems of the 1980s and 1990s meant that less money was available for health care. Expansion of health facilities has not kept up with population growth, especially in the towns. Access to clinics and to medicine is still difficult for the poor and those living in rural areas.

divided into three years of junior secondary and three of senior. Subjects are taught in English.

In the 1960s Nigeria had only two universities, but today all major towns have universities and other higher education institutions such as teacher training colleges and colleges of agriculture. Current enrollment in these colleges is estimated at between 150,000 and 200,000.

Other, older systems also exist alongside Western-style education: Islamic education and informal education are examples.

Islamic education is the oldest system of formal education in western Africa. Muslim children often attend Koranic schools as well as their state primary

Life in Rural Areas

In rural areas most Nigerians live by farming and some trading. The network of roads throughout Nigeria and the great expansion of education have brought changes to village life, but many aspects of daily life stay the same.

In the rural northern areas, most Hausa people dwell in family compounds, where three generations of a family may live together. Houses are made of bricks covered with clay and have thatch roofs. Beautiful patterns often decorate the walls. Around the compound a wall or fence provides privacy. Visitors enter the compound through a *zaure* (ZOW-ree), a reception room. In the compound there may be a small garden for growing vegetables, some fruit trees, and a granary for keeping grain. Many villages now have piped water, but there will probably also be a well. Muslim men are allowed up to four wives. Each wife has her own room, but they all share the same kitchen.

Most families have some farmland, growing crops for household use and to sell. The men do most of the farming, especially if their wives are in purdah. They often keep a few livestock such as goats, sheep, cattle, or hens.

The Igbo people of eastern Nigeria all lived in villages until recently, when many moved to towns and cities. Each Igbo village forms part of a group of small villages, all built close together. At the heart of each village stands the meeting center; paths, cleared from the forest, radiate out from here like the rays of the

A family compound in the Hausa city of Zaria. Thick mud walls keep the rooms inside cool. The elaborate patterns beautify the outside of the family home.

A traditional house with a thatched roof and grass walls in the Niger Delta region. In this area of wetlands and rivers, many people survive by fishing for their food.

culture. The delta is a patchwork of creeks and mangrove swamps. Areas of dry land are quite small. Most people live by fishing, and they often travel between villages by boat. Small areas of land are cleared for farming and building houses. People grow yams and cassava. In recent years the government has encouraged them to grow rice.

The Niger Delta produces oil, the source of much of Nigeria's recent wealth. This has had a huge impact on people's lives, although few of the local people have benefited from it. In recent years unrest has increased. The villagers say that the oil has polluted their waters and poisoned the fish.

sun. Family compounds are scattered along these paths. Each family has their own compound with mud walls around it. Many houses are still made of mud; newer houses have zinc roofs.

People's lives center on farming, trading, and keeping small stores or stalls. The Igbo grow many different vegetables, but yams are the most important crop.

All Igbo families in a village are related to one another. The oldest man in the family is head of the household. Traditionally he is allowed several wives, but today most Igbo are Christian and men have only one wife. When children are young, they sleep and eat with their mother. As they grow up, they separate. Boys eat with their father and girls with their mother.

The peoples of the Niger Delta, including the Ijaw (EE-jaw) and Ibibio (ih-BEE-bee-oe), are related to the Igbo by language and

A Nomadic Way of Life

The Fulani people live mostly in the north. Some have settled in towns and villages, while others are nomadic, roaming across the dry savanna with their herds of cattle and sheep.

The Fulani nomads' way of life is unique in Nigeria. They are constantly on the move in small groups, setting up camp near the best pastures. Their life is a demanding one, yet they regard their lifestyle superior to the the settled lifestyle of the people whose villages and towns they pass through.

Cattle are at the heart of Fulani life. They rarely kill a cow for its meat, preferring to live on the milk and butter produced. Fulani cattle are large and certainly not docile, yet each cow is given a name, and boys learn when they are very young how to keep a large herd under control.

Life in the Towns and Cities

Families make their homes in the most basic shelters on the edge of a Lagos garbage dump. For the poorest of the poor, living conditions are harsh.

Living in towns and cities has been a way of life for many Nigerians, especially among the Hausa and the Yoruba, for hundreds of years. However, urban areas have grown rapidly in recent years. It is estimated that by 2010 more than 40 percent of all of Nigeria's people will live in towns.

The largest of these towns is Lagos with a population of more than six million. Lagos used to be the capital of Nigeria, until the government built a brand new capital at Abuja (ah-BOO-jah), right in the geographical heart of the country. However, Lagos remains Nigeria's main city, a place Nigerians both love and hate, where millions have flocked to seek their fortune. It boasts impressive modern buildings, expensive hotels, and smart shops. It also has the worst traffic jams imaginable, open sewers, and appalling living conditions for the majority of its people. Many people do whatever they can to survive. The poorest pick from the great piles of garbage to find something worth keeping or selling. Crime and corruption are rife. Much of Lagos doesn't work. The electricity supply is unreliable, and during the rains the roads are almost impassable. In spite of all this, Lagos pulses with energy and vitality, and its streets are full of people, wandering animals, cars, trucks, and buses.

Kano (KAH-noe), at the very opposite end of the country, is a very different city. Almost on the fringes of the Sahara, it is hot, dry, and dusty. Kano has been an important Hausa city for hundreds of years. Today it is still the largest of the towns and cities of northern Nigeria. The old city, like the towns of Katsina and Zaria, is surrounded by mud walls. Inside stand

people live in towns, many quite small; others, such as Ibadan (ee-bah-DAHN) and Ilorin (ee-LOE-reen), are much larger. Most people still live in family compounds, but these houses look different from the traditional mud-brick and thatch. Most houses are two-storied, with zinc roofs, and many have electricity and piped water.

Although they live in towns, many Yoruba families still own farms. They may have to travel for several hours by bus or by car to reach their land.

As Muslim men leave a mosque after Friday prayers in the old city of Kano, beggars ask for alms. All Muslims are expected to give money to the poor.

Food in Great Variety

Many types of food are eaten in Nigeria. However, for their main meal of the day, most Nigerians eat a staple food, such as yam, cassava, or rice, accompanied by a

many family compounds, narrow streets, mosques, small stores, and markets. In the old days there were separate areas for specialized artisans, such as cloth dyers and weavers, and for "strangers"—non-Hausa, often non-Muslim peoples attracted by the wealth and trade of Kano.

Outside the small area of the old city lies the modern city of Kano, with its international airport, government buildings, and urban sprawl. Even in this modern part of the city, Kano has a distinctive feel, with many Hausa men in their long, flowing gowns, the old and new mosques, and the busy markets.

In western Nigeria most of the Yoruba

Refreshments at a wedding party in Benin City in southern Nigeria. Wedding guests, dressed in their finest clothes, are offered beer, soft drinks, and snacks.

sauce containing meat or fish with vegetables. Sauces are usually flavored with onions, tomatoes, and hot peppers. The meat may be chicken, beef, mutton, or goat. In the south people eat pork, but Muslims are forbidden to eat any meat from the pig. Wealthier families will have meat in almost all their sauces. In the south a giant land snail is regarded as a delicacy.

Vegetables are widely grown and used in different recipes. They include okra (a green vegetable also known as ladies' fingers because of its shape), spinach, and plantain (a large kind of banana that is usually fried). Other popular ingredients include dried cowpeas, peanuts, and *egusi* (ae-GOO-see). Egusi comes from dried melon or pumpkin seeds. The shell is taken off and the nut is ground up to add taste and thickness to sauces.

Nigerians love to snack—when traveling, shopping in markets, and at parties. Two favorite snacks are made from cowpeas that are boiled and then mashed up: *akkras* (AH-krahs), a fried bean cake, and *moi-moi* (MOY-moy), which is wrapped and steamed. Roasted corn, plantain chips, and roasted salted peanuts are also popular.

Nigerian fruits vary according to season and include oranges, bananas, mangoes, guavas, and papayas. Soft drinks and beer are very popular, mostly made and bottled locally. In the south palm wine is a favorite drink.

Nigerians often chew kola nut, a slightly bitter nut that has a mild stimulant effect. Kola nut is especially popular among Muslims, who are forbidden to drink alcohol.

Dress: Caftans and Wrappers

In the north the men wear long gowns called *rigas* (REE-gahz) or caftans over pants. For special occasions, such as a wedding or party, men also wear finely embroidered caps. In the south men wear gowns known as *agbada* (ahg-BAH-dah), which are usually more brightly colored or have more dramatic patterns than those worn in the north. Western dress is worn as well but is more popular in the south.

For women, the most popular form of dress is a blouse combined with a wrapper, a piece of cloth tied at the waist. It is comfortable and cool, the perfect dress for a hot climate. Wrappers come in all kinds of patterns and materials, ranging from simple cotton for everyday use to fine lace for special occasions. Women also often wear head ties: from simple scarves to big, elaborate head ties.

A weaver making cloth on a traditional loom. Much cloth is now imported from overseas, but the distinctive patterns and colors of handwoven cloth remain popular.

The Ogun Festival

Yoruba festivals are held to celebrate different gods. Although many Yoruba people are now Christian (and some are Muslim), they regard the festivals as an important part of their history and culture.

The Ogun Festival is held each year in September and celebrates the Yoruba god of war. The celebrations last all day, with processions of dancers and drummers. Many dancers wear fierce-looking disguises.

Everyone dresses in their best clothes, gives presents to each other, and shares food. Many Yoruba people believe that if they do not celebrate the Ogun Festival properly, a year of disaster will follow.

Protected from the heat of the sun by a colorful parasol, a priest takes part in the annual Yoruba festival to celebrate Ogun, the god of war, metals, and metalworkers.

Nigerian Art: From Calabashes to Cement

Nigeria has a rich heritage in arts and crafts, ranging from things crafted for everyday use, such as raffia baskets, decorated calabashes and pots, to the beautiful carvings and sculptures made by highly skilled artisans.

In the past certain crafts were closely linked to religion. Wood-carvers and bronze casters were believed to have magical powers through the products they created. Today much of that religious significance has gone, and the quality of such work has suffered as a result.

However, many modern artists work in Nigeria today. Drawing on tradition, they also absorb influences from the outside world. They may work in a wide range of materials, including aluminum and cement. The work of artists such as Ashiru Olatunde, who works with aluminum and other media to depict Yoruba life, and Adebisi Akanji, who sculpts large-scale works with vivid scenes of everyday

Nigerian life, has international appeal yet remains uniquely Nigerian.

Imported and factory-made goods are often more highly prized than local crafts. Yet craftsmanship still thrives throughout much of Nigeria. The most widespread crafts are weaving, pottery, leather work, calabash carving, and textile work—weaving, dyeing, and printing.

Nigerians love decoration and color, and these appear on almost everything. Truck drivers will commission an artist to decorate their truck and paint slogans, such as In God We Trust, designed to reassure their passengers on the crowded, badly kept Nigerian roads traveled by poor drivers.

Music and Dance

Music and dance are essential to most Nigerians. Music can be divided into traditional music and modern pop music. Traditional music is found more in the villages and pop music in the towns, although there is no rigid division and modern musicians may often mix both styles. Traditional music and dance usually have a special purpose. There are different kinds for baptisms, weddings, and funerals; for chiefs; for women and men; and for hunters and warriors. Each ethnic group in Nigeria also has its own unique style of dance, and Nigerians hardly need an excuse to get up and move.

Pop music is more for entertainment, especially for dancing. The most famous Nigerian musicians in recent years have been Fela Anikulapo Kuti and "King" Sunny Ade. Kuti, who died in 1997, was one of Africa's most famous, and controversial, musicians. He frequently spoke out against the government and was sent to prison for his critical views. With

Traditional Yoruba musicians play to the crowds in the streets of Ilorin in western Nigeria. Here, the main instruments include drums and simple, but loud, horns.

lyrics that argued for the rights of ordinary men and women, his music blended African rhythms and American jazz; he called it "Afro-beat." Ade plays a kind of music known as *juju* (JOO-joo). His band, the African Beats, has between twenty and thirty musicians and vocalists, who combine fine vocal harmonies, electric guitars, and traditional instruments such as the talking drum, which imitates the sound of human speach.

Oral and Written Stories

Nigerians have always had a great love of storytelling. Legends, poems, songs, and stories have been handed down through the generations. This store of oral literature is complemented today by written literature, including the novels of Chinua Achebe, Cyprian Ekwensi, Ben Okri, and Buchi Emecheta and the plays of Wole Soyinka. Soyinka recently won the Nobel Prize for Literature. He also campaigns for human rights in Nigeria and has been sent to jail and into exile for his views.

Many other writers are active but unknown. They are the anonymous authors of books called *onitsha* (oh-NEET-shah), which are produced and sold very cheaply. Most of these books are written in Pidgin and tell colorful tales of Nigerian life.

Popular Sports

In Nigeria, as in other countries in Africa, soccer is an obsession. The Nigerian national soccer team, the Super Eagles, have won an Olympic gold medal and were one of the favorites for the 1998 World Cup. That same year, the Nigerian Women's Team, the Super Falcons, dominated the African Women's Soccer Championships.

The annual Hausa fishing festival at Argungu (ahr-GOON-goo). Fishermen use large floating calabashes, hollowed from gourds, to hold the fish they catch.

In the past wrestling was probably the most widely practiced and most popular spectator sport. Even today, village wrestling matches are events in which everyone is caught up in the excitement. Wrestlers often fight in teams, accompanied by drumming. Younger boys fight first, leading up to the climax when the champion wrestlers come on.

A Hausa man, dressed as a warrior, decorates his horse for the Sallah celebrations, where men on horseback gallop in mock battle charges before the emir.

Sallah, a Muslim Festival

The Hausa and Fulani peoples are Muslim. Their festivals are known as sallahs (suh-LAHZ), and the greatest of all the sallahs comes at the end of Ramadan. This is the month of fasting, when Muslims must not eat or drink between sunrise and sunset. When the new moon appears, Muslims know that the fast can end and the celebrations and feasting begin.

During the day, a procession proceeds between the palace of the emir, or chief, and the mosque. Everyone dresses in their best clothes and comes out to greet the emir. The procession includes hunters, dancers, praise singers, drummers, and trumpeters. Men dress in the robes of warriors and lead mock charges on horseback. At the heart of the procession rides the emir on his finest horse.

Afterward, families and friends return to their homes to share food. Special dishes are cooked for a celebration meal. Poorer families, who can't afford meat on a regular basis, might butcher a cow or goat. Sallah is a day for everyone to enjoy, and it also helps people to remember the importance of their own history and culture.

Glossary

Afrikaner: any South African person of European descent who speaks Afrikaans (a language developed from Dutch) as a first language.

apprentice: someone, usually a young woman or man, who works for a skilled person in order to learn their trade or craft. An apprenticeship may last for several years.

bankrupt: not having enough money to pay your debts.

bauxite: a mineral from which aluminum is made.

boycott: to refuse to have any contact with a person or an organization. Boycotts are often a way of protesting against a government or a political policy.

caftan: a long, loose gown, usually made of cotton or silk and worn to keep cool in hot climates. Caftans are worn mostly by men in the Middle East and in parts of Africa.

cassava: a plant with fleshy tuber roots, used as a food.

CFA franc: franc de la Communauté Financière Africaine (franc of the African Financial Community). This is a unit of currency shared by various African countries that were formerly French colonies.

columbite: a mineral compound, black in color.

communism: a theory that suggests that all property belongs to the community and that work should be organized for the common good.

communist: someone who believes in the theory of communism.

compulsory: enforced, often by law.

coup: a change of government brought about by force.

escarpment: the steep face or cliff of a mountain ridge or range of hills.

European Union: an alliance of European nations committed to economic union and closer political integration. It developed out of the European Economic Community (founded in 1957).

fundamentalist: in religion, someone who believes that everything in the holy scriptures is the literal truth.

gastric: of or to do with the stomach or digestion. Symptoms of gastric illnesses include diarrhea, vomiting, dehydration (loss of body fluid), and fever.

graphite: a type of carbon, which is soft, greasy, and black or gray. This mineral is used to make pencil lead and lubricants.

human rights abuses: human rights are conditions that many people believe are deserved by all human beings, such as freedom, equality, or justice. Abuses are acts that deny people such rights. Examples of abuses might include torture, censorship, or imprisonment without trial.

Koran: the holy book of Islam.

Koranic schools: classrooms attached to mosques (buildings where Muslim people pray). Boys go there to learn how to read Arabic and to study the faith of Islam.

malaria: a disease spread by mosquitoes. It may cause fever, unconsciousness, and death.

mandate: an authorization granted by the League of Nations (or its successor, the United Nations) to one of its member countries to govern a conquered territory.

millet: a hardy cereal crop grown for food, drink, and fodder.

monopoly: sole control of a market, without competition.

oracle: a place, usually a religious shrine, where a person could ask a god for help in times of trouble. The god's answer was often communicated through a priest or priestess.

pneumonia: a disease of the lungs caused by infection or irritants.

regime: a form of government.

republic: a government in which power resides in a body of elected representatives.

rife: widespread or common, often referring to something bad.

savanna: a grassland dotted with trees and drought-resistant undergrowth.

socialism: a political theory in which the community as a whole controls land, property, industry, and money, and organizes them for the good of all the people.

socialist: someone who believes in the theory of socialism.

sorghum: a grain crop commonly grown in hot countries.

subsistence farming: growing crops for one's own use rather than selling them.

taboo: an object or an activity that is forbidden by religion or social custom.

terra-cotta: unglazed, brown-red pottery.

theology: the study of religion and of religious ideas and beliefs.

tuberculosis: a disease of the tissues in the human body, especially those in the lungs.

typhoid: a disease caused by germs in polluted water. It causes severe vomiting and diarrhea.

Further Reading

Internet Sites

Look under Countries A to Z in the Atlapedia Online Web Site at
   http://www.atlapedia.com/online/countries
Look under country listing in the CIA World Factbook Web Site at
   http://www.odci.gov/cia/publications/factbook
Look under country listing in the Library of Congress Country Studies Web Site at
   http://lcweb2.loc.gov/frd/cs/cshome.html

Morocco

Blauer, Ettagale, and Jason Laure. *Morocco.* Broomall, PA: Chelsea House, 2000.
Hermes, Jules M. *The Children of Morocco.* Minneapolis, MN: Lerner Group, 1995.
Seward, Pat. *Morocco.* Tarrytown, NY: Benchmark Books, 1995.

Mozambique

James, R. S. *Mozambique.* Broomall, PA: Chelsea House, 1997.
Johnson, Robert, Jr., and Gary Van Wyk. *Shona.* New York: Rosen Group, 1996.
Lauré, Jason, and Ettagale Blauer. *Mozambique.* Danbury, CT Children's Press. 1997.

Namibia

Bernard, Alan. *Kalahari Bushmen.* Orlando, FL: Raintree Steck-Vaughn, 1994.
Biesele, Megan, and Kxao Loloo. *San.* New York: Rosen Group, 1996.
Brandenberg, Jim. *Sand and Fog: Adventures in Southern Africa.* New York: Walker & Company, 1996.
Lauré, Jason, and Ettagale Blauer. *Namibia.* Danbury, CT: Children's Press. 1997.
Udechukwu, Ada U. *Herero.* New York: Rosen Group, 1996.

Niger

Adeleke, Tunde. *Songhay.* New York: Rosen Group, 1996.
Ndukwe, Pat I. *Fulani.* New York: Rosen Group, 1995.
Parris, Ronald G. *Hausa.* New York: Rosen Group, 1996.
Seffal, Robah. *Niger.* Tarrytown, NY: Benchmark Books, 2000.

Nigeria

Anda, Michael O. *Yoruba.* New York: Rosen Group, 1996.
Azuonye, Chukwuma. *Edo: The Bini People of the Benin Kingdom.* New York: Rosen Group, 1996.
Berg, Elizabeth. *Nigeria.* Milwaukee, WI: Gareth Stevens, 1998.
Freville, Nicholas. *Nigeria.* Broomall, PA: Chelsea House, 2000.
Levy, Patricia Marjorie. *Nigeria.* Tarrytown, NY: Benchmark Books, 1996.
Ndukwe, Pat I. *Fulani.* New York: Rosen Group, 1995.
Ogbaa, Kalu. *Igbo.* New York: Rosen Group, 1995.
Owhonda, John. *Nigeria: A Nation of Many Peoples.* Minneapolis, MN: Dillon Press, 1997.
Parris, Ronald G. *Hausa.* New York: Rosen Group, 1996.
Sutherland, D. *Nigeria.* Danbury, CT: Grolier Educational Corporation, 1997.
Tenquist, Alasdair. *Nigeria.* Detroit, MI: Thomson Learning, 1996.

Index

Page numbers in *italic* indicate illustrations.

Page numbers in *italic* indicate illustrations.